Love Hangs Upon an Empty Door

The Poetry of Bruce Wright

Barricade Books, Inc. New York

Published by Barricade Books Inc.
150 Fifth Avenue
New York, NY 10011

Design and page layout by Jeff Nordstedt

Printed in the United States of America

Library of Congress Cataloging-in-Publication Data

Wright, Bruce. 1918-
    Love hangs upon an empty door : the poetry of Bruce
    Wright.
        p.   cm.
    ISBN 1-56980-129-0
    I. Title.
PS3573.R494L6   1998   98-24616
811' .54--dc21   CIP

For my father not in heaven, Rev. Lawrence Lucas,

Bruce Wright
4/2/99

Dedication

To all of the women who have made them-
selves and Paris the greatest joys of my life.

Contents

Introduction

On August 29, 1998, the *New York Times* published a profile of Bruce M. Wright by Joyce Wadler. The article was written after Judge Wright and I lunched with Ms. Wadler at Londel's Restaurant in Harlem.

During that lunch conversation, I said to Joyce Wadler, "You should walk through the streets of Harlem with this guy. He's a folk hero."

And indeed he is.

From the day I met Judge Wright, more than a decade ago, I recognized him as an unusual man in many ways. He is truly an original—an atheist not afraid to express his atheism. A rebel against injustice who speaks out regardless of consequences.

As a Judge, he was unique. His decisions were the result of careful research, keen understanding and often brilliant approaches leading to fair results.

My company published two of his books of prose. *Black Robes; White Justice* was enthusiastically praised by the critics. His recent memoir, *Black Justice in a White World* has been highly acclaimed. It recounts tales of his life in Paris where he went AWOL during World War II because of his disgust with the segregation in our armed forces.

Over the course of our friendship, I often, heard Judge Wright say, "I think of myself as a poet."

So, when my wife turned to me one day and said, "Do you know what we have to do? We must publish a collection of Bruce's poetry."

You don't fight with your wife.

And so it was and so here it is. These pages contain a selection of those poems Judge Wright believes are his best.

In that *New York Times* article quoted above, Judge Wright remarked that he would prefer to be remembered as a poet.

"The law has not civilized America," he said. "Poetry might."

Welcome to the thoughtful, perceptive, challenging and often moving world of the poetry of Bruce Wright.

Lyle Stuart
New York City
September 1998

Notes On A Late Lamented Statesman

Having read carefully the selected letters of a late
Tormented statesman (his diary had been suppressed for
One Hundred years by the family of a former mistress),
I felt some of the pressures of a by-gone civics,
Saw twice-told some of the impolitic gossip of diplomacy
And discerned the natural conflict
Between well-to-do id and Christian purpose.
For those who peered behind the curtains of the print,
There were blurs, gaps and imperfect bridges,
For the man wrote with the vision of greatness in his pen
And with history as his hoped-for Pantheon.
An isolated poetic expression, now and then,
Was his obvious reach for an elusive depth,
A consciousness of the meaning of his meaning,
Of his existence, his quest for a throne for conscience.

No speechwriter or Thesaurus had preened his private syntax,
However, and having known him in every fashion of his
Emperor's Clothing,
It was a reading stutter to leap across the vital gaps,
The vacant recesses he could not fill with heroic
Bronzes of himself. His careful phrases sought to dramatize
Each post-scripted after-thought, and it was the excessive
Taking care which erased the burning temper of a proper
Biography and yielded to his ego the kind of polish which
Obscures, but does not heal the lasting blemish.

Clearly, these were not confessions to endanger
Augustine or Rousseau, for they never dared to examine
Personal excreta or the foolish census of social institutions.
He nevertheless seemed to know that certain documents of
Proportion and modesty must not give way to his felt italics,
Lest there be revealed such secrets as the latter-day
Sexual comforts and discomforts of his different drumming,
His now-I-lay-me-downs.

Politicians think a nominee should be a diplomatic missionary
    and an expert
If he can mispronounce with sincere grace and the humor of it all
Those fairy tale names and places
Of the far-geography his country's money seeks to aid.
The senators who must endow his appointment as a national trust,
Seemed to wish to believe he shared the foresight of
His father's commerce among certain primitive races;
After all, it was the father's fiscal tact which had managed to
Extract from tea, tin and distant sweat, the makings of
An Alger hero's fortune. There were some expressions of awe
And open admiration for the tax-aware complexities of the
    foundation
To which the nominee had consigned his shares and municipal exempts.
But the applause after his swearing-in, had sounded a rude acoustic,
Even then, like opera sung in English.
His expressions of faith in a harmonious and unified
Commercial discipline of well-run business ecumenics,
Had been based upon his study of old-time Baedekers;
But how rare he had been in being both correct and right,
Where every other Oracle and Sphinx had failed.

He expressed quite simply, for example, the opaque distinctions
Between agrarian reform and the subversion of Christian peoples
Under the corruptions of Marx, and he knew, as well, all of
The Chiang-Kai-Shek shortcomings and even some
Of MacArthur's burnished flaws and patriotic faults.
His personal data had become public, in the way that
Tailored subjects and predicates become proper adjectives
And flatter the past. Just so.

In solemn word and cautious punctuation,
His symmetry emerged in guided print.
The profile and substance of a man of peace, one United Nations
Claque noted. An international fiscal alliance was our hope,
He said. And he made this seem the hard currency
Of a remarkable insight.
He urged favorable detentes, geopolitical and social compacts
(He had read a son's first-year text-book on English philosophers),
And he felt SALT should abolish some arms, not just limit them,

He knew, also, what teasing hints to suggest, what
Historical lash to flick,
What clues to whet an inference and not reveal,
For there must always be a turning up of time's candle-wick
To flare against the Lincolnesque barrens of poverty
And to shine upon a close reading of the classics.

The names of his power friends were moved as in a game of
    tactics and he
Walked among them as a public penitent confessing long-time virtue
For the scholars of his ruins. Never betrayed were the private
Parts of personal intrigue, or the feral mercies of ambition,
Lest history be crippled and studied less,
And the un-written shilling shocker revealed as truth after all,
Or he emerge as just plain and human. But such humanity must not
Be found in the bed-time failings, or in some unsolved moral
    mystery.
In any case, there would always be detractors,
Even (as he always said), of Christ,
He was wary of those meretricious probers, who somehow defied
Those frightened in junctions against publishing diaries;
But muck will be raked, and it never fails to discover in
The commerce of strange bedrooms, sensations for the mob.

It was enough that he remembered condemnations for those
Who sought to force a familiar profile from what
He called the cozened darkness of Ohio's Blooming Grove, for
    example,
Where the shape of an ethnic scandal confided
To America's astonished hearsay that there was once a
Part-Black President, knowing that the American ethnic formula
Means Negro.
I knew something of his torment. It was painful to share.
Today, however, one likes to think the times are different
And that even one-time bigots try to care.

ii

The committees of our Congress are impressed by wealth
And they applaud one's divestiture of securities,
As though the owner of such engraved paper is
Horatius at that Tiber bridge, and their own.

Except for the Major Powers, self-appointed, guardians,
and who, after all, in the West, had discovered
The benevolent uses of destruction and benign neglect.
He shuddered aloud at press conferences
And was heard forthrightly to express the fear
That Germany might one day seek to launch another Thousand Years.

In a manner he said was not intended to appall the gritty agitations
In the Middle East,
He worried about the twentieth century diaspora discovering Israel
And making European miracles among the scatterings of Araby.
He felt it better to placate the good earth's oil. Without
Naming a trespasser, he voiced concern about intrusions
Upon ancient lands where Christ had trod. His father,
He said, had known quite well, the reticence of the First
Earl of Balfour, and he had personally once stayed for a night
At a timeless inn in Palestine. Not even Apartheid was obscure
To his family's famous notice, for a theme of World Community
Infused his speeches (he was a beardless guru of a solar dream
Of perfect politics, a Third World radical had joked);
But mothers of boys and wives of men who, he said, must be
Brought back to their star-spangled home from their conflict
In remote latitudes, sang hosannas for his vision
And their plaques and parchments were grateful writings on
  his wall.

iii

Out-raced by a distant focus never caught,
His obituary began in headlines of The Times.
Bachrach, the taxidermist for the famed and rich,
Claimed credit for the three-columned photo
(Made some years ago, a small note reminded);
But putting aside the vanity of playing tricks upon time,
One felt that Aristotle must have regarded the head of Homer so;
It showed that handsome prime so much needed for his doings
In his father's name. His private negotiations were touched upon,
As messages from both royalty and primitive leaders were quoted.

Such recollections formalized a national grief. He had been
But sixty-two. As with Washington, the father of America, He
  had no children;

None, that is, who could rise from rumor and place a legal mortgage
On his name. His distances had included his nearest kin;
They were tangential extensions in their long wait,
But they were experts in tenuous geneology and the ties of cousinship,
As they quickly asserted their twice-removed status
To claim the trusts which held his stocks and bonds;
For them, not even the municipals were exempt.

One, emphasizing certain dimpled similarities, produced
A joyous picture on a private beach, a picnic,
Where God was flesh and walking upon behaving seas.
Another survivor, not to be out-done
By such documents of heirship, pointed to a framed enlargement
Of the past, purporting to show a reunion of loving strangers.
Retrospect became fouled in financed fealty to the dead.
The Government, much deprived,
Allowed its most graceful writers to author a suitable
Death biography. With that poetry of praise which specializes in
Epitaphs for the worthy and the unworthy,
It was said that humanity had been diminished by his absent
    mediation.

The haughty banners of allies in grief were lowered half-way
Down their masts; it was a sign of the times that, on that day,
The wind had no zest. But there was a military funeral,
Complete with baffled horses, a bare saddle and invisible rider,
In the way that great generals are certified by public sorrow,
Even though light brigades have long-since been charged by tanks.
There were some empty boots, turned backwards in their ambiguity;
There they were, strapped into polished stirrups.

We who knew him, knew that he never cared for horses.
However, the dirges were noble,
And from that hardy era when commanders named their steeds
For places both had survived in the doing of their deeds.
The band was smart and integrated, with state funerals its sole
    duty.
It honored ethnic amendments moreso than the corpse it dirged.
For the induced moment of official sadness, it seemed better
Not to know what his diary had omitted,
Or what his married mistress had in hers.

Senegal Revisited

The tongues of America now pronounce
the Slavic resonance of Poland
as Wocziehowicz is made a part of Michigan,
while priests intone a monologue from Rome;
muezzins and the ram's horn merge
with steeple bells,
bringing sacred babble
to the diaspora of every Standish and their
Priscillas,
scattering different mayflowers across
America's stolen land;
where once canterbury's allegiance
exacted the Protestant vow,
there are now many mansions of mystery;
nor have the lips of African imports
and ex-slave syllables of a gemmed geography
of our exiled home escaped the impudence
of Malcolm-X,
who once fled without a country
and returned to the noisy echo
of his ghetto Samara.
Nice Negroes never die that way,
although funerals remain the same, whether
in the pentecostal weeping for the dead,
or in Harlem made the flesh and blood of Islam.

ii

But why is my made-up name and who is my tribe?
Thrust from the crippled foetus of three-fifths,
I am convicted, doomed to sail this dry land
a boatless Philip Nolan;
and yet, I feel the illness of the sea,
for even now, sometimes, the Atlantic seems
    transfused
splashing red on all my abolitions
as it washes tidal graves in cemeteries

14

beneath its waves.
Walking the water,
these fearful repetitions of the long-since dead
are my million ghosts of Banquo,
too distant and too drowned
to be cared for in their soggy ash
by Sunday visits to Atlantis,
their bones merged with fish-patterns
in unbottomed depths.

I should have only dreamed my Middle Passage
relationships: Instead, I went to Africa
where I could see a black President
and argue in his noble house.
There, an independent banner
has transmuted native sons;
it was a strange La Mancha from where to
start my search,
that one-time place and market for my father's flesh-
all my fathers. I searched for the darkness
of their ancient and captured time,
their shackled tether.
I searched in the dust of alien museums,
longing for translations of the hard songs
        and strange dialects;
Oh, how I searched among the familiar shapes
        and colors that were no different from my own,
but those foreign faces uttered the rough gutterals
of Araby as they strode in the symmetries
of Trinidad, Montserrat, Harlem, the profiles
of Grenada, St. Lucia, Nevis and all the
        Windwards;
but I could place no genetic mortgage
on buried kingdoms or princes of the past;
I cowered in the heedless sun,
looking upon the scorch of burning bushes,
begging them to make the bible talk,
and all the while, kinship kept a doubtful rhythm,
as pulse and heartbeat stuttered out of time.

I met a guide who was anxious to show me
where the captured slaves were once chained
before they embarked upon an un-sought tryst.
He could have been my brother.
He seemed not to sweat in his European suit and tie
and he smiled out a pride of tribal history in French;
he pointed to the now sanitary dungeons
from where black caravans sailed upon a
        Westward tide;
my nude beginnings were now washed and posed,
postures for the focus of Instamatic tourists,
grist for Polaroids and colored slides,
or the murder gossip told by my cultivated guide
whose lips betrayed the arrogance of a smile
as he recited his cleansed history and facts,
like an eager student recalling
weathers of the past.

I looked towards Jamestown
across the heaving sickness of the sea
and wondered how the guide and I
had both returned to this shackled port,
he from the Sorbonne and I from places I could
neither leave nor love.

In that place of fiery sun, I felt un-hinged
to have bought a visa for that land,
but there we stood,
caught up in a common circumstance of race
as the equator burned down upon us both.

I stared at the iron manacles embedded
in the wall of the island of slaves;
time fell out of season;
the guide's voice became entangled in the
        woody vines
and crimson blood of local flowers;
peculiar institutions had become
smiling conquests for his travelogue excesses.
I was reminded of undertakers

16

sweetly urging satin comforts for the dead:
I walked away, followed by his syllables;
I sat deep within the shade of a withered baobab
and drowned my tears with sweat.

After the harsh fact of a visit to the island of Gorée, off the coast of Dakar and actually touching the rusted shackles that detained kidnapped Africans while they waited for a favorable tide.

Estate Nazareth, an old slave plantation,
Secret Harbour, St. Thomas
Virgin Islands, circa 1972.

Mother's Day

Mother Africa, across the sea
I cannot hear your call to me;
Your brilliant sun, exotic plants,
Your folkloric and barefoot dance,
Your National Geographic nudes
Rebuking well-clad Christian prudes,
Don't attract my leer or ogle
And no matter how my eyes may boggle
When viewing the origins of the Nile,
I can't forget the fatal bile
That spurred the Ibo and the Hausa
Into strife and *mortis causa*
Who with the gun and sharp machete
Engaged disputes, both great and petty,
That profanes Uganda's waters
With dead Rwandan sons and daughters,
That gives Liberia's plains and shores
The decimation of itself in wars;
That watches Angola count its dead,
And the dark Sudan guillotines its head.

Lufwalnu Nabru-Orgen
The Year of the Viper.

18

Love places its victims on emotional welfare rolls.

Evol Hab.

Love is the mating of two sewer systems.

Palinurus

Love is [sometimes.]

Lufwalnu Nabru-Orgen

e·n·d·i·n·g·s

For Yvette: May 20, 1937
March 12, 1966

That I have loved that woman
captured now behind the shrouds of canvas curtain,
scalpels out at memory of other beds.
The doctor, a prophylactic snowman, an icy statue,
gestures to condemn me away;
I am not of his calling
and now have no claim upon the body and the blood
now his.
My eyes trouble as I hear his movements,
his scientific trespass
touching where I have slept and tasted.
Drinking tears, I fumble at a book;
the words stutter;
the title reverses time and place;
'I think of her request for Simone de Beauvoir
as she recalled her own memoirs of a dutiful daughter;
she had smiled at her recollection of her kneeling
days of devotion at the Church of St. Martin de Porres,
her days of obligation.
"I paid duty and imported nothing,"
she would joke, recalling her confirmation
and how sometimes she remarked how her Hail-Marys
could never make her an acolyte
or custodian of the candle fire.

It was later that she realized and dared doubt
to mention how The Word becomes snared upon its
        limits;
she toyed with the heresy of God as woman
and invented new definitions for morals
and, of course, sin.

She had once jokingly thought of Paris as a temptation
from the strictures of the natural law;

20

the City of Light had become her unseen mirror of
    amazement,
and the tales of the war years that I told
worried at her Roman fundamentals.

The doctor, advised by microscopic clues,
was a stern Oracle refusing questions;
he did, however, bid me to be cheerful, prescribing
avoidance of the predicates and treasoned craft of doom.

A nurse admonished me to wear the false face
of easy confidence and cheer
and so, risking fragile humor,
I pat her pillow, adjust the bed and ask
if the probers respect her royal blood
that once owned a Congo claim
upon the darkness in her veins.

It was a question of ashes I sought to swallow.

A Dracula of healing hovered
ready to plunge a greedy needle into an arm
that had always astonished by its grace of slim muscle.
Slaking at the crimson passion of her life,
the deed was done. Lady Macbeth, R. N.,
smiled and moved on with her warm loot.

I could feed her, an aide whispered.
It was a plate of bland,
an offering of unleavened flavor.
But hungers were elsewhere.
Other beds,
other ways.

In rooms of ebbing life, one's nose
is bludgeoned by the sanitary reek of illness,
and those who are well
are embarrassed by their health,
and they curse internally,
fend at guilt and pretend there
is no anxiety to leave, or how.

She smiles in her shrunken jeopardy,
taunting thoughts
that once bound our joy to the same bed.
Love sometimes bangs upon an empty door
as we see life in all its dazzling colors
become discarded wrappings from a lost gift.

ii

I marvel at the bedside seers
costumed in their starched immunity,
with their stethoscopes and Latin mixtures;
they presume to know our secret statistics,
the source of our red fluid,
how much to siphon from where and when
and how one pain refers its torture to another.

She sees my discomfort and summons a smile.
She could not see the deadly notes the interns
    made,
or hear their consultations, their lectures
and their focus on the faint graph of her survival.
The doctors measured their doses,
as false as Hallowe'en devices;
the pills shown in their colorwheel array,
placebos pumped into her pause along the road to
Samara.

She sleeps. I sit. She stirs. I waver.
I stare, a watchman for disaster, ready to cry out
and help her summon salvation
from her Vatican totems.
I speak softly of the ribboned flowers
sent by clients whose concerns nag her to be well;
awake, she moves her lips
as though confiding to her Rosary;
she becomes a Muse of speculation about Caribbean
weathers
and she speaks of the long rest she will take.
Impossibilities are always worthy of their mention,
like remembering what never was, or counting

promises that are the need of self-deception,
intentions that end their lives before our own.
We always envision the past as worthy of resurrection
and forget its grimace of harsh regret;
memory sometimes slashes beyond our depths
and gives us the fraud to renovate dead vows
until they sink three times at once.

iii

"The parquet floor deserves a quiet pattern. Speak
to your Armenian friend." She suddenly
thought of her living room, lying there in that clinic
      for the dying.
As though in a domestic conference,
we spoke of the pewter on our mantel piece
and how the landlord must be called
about the misconduct of the chimney smoke;
she spoke of the books at random on the floor
spilling their subjects all about.
"They should be catalogued," she smiled.
It reminded me of P. G. Wodehouse, his library
plots and country homes we would never have.

One friend had sent his own arrangement of
her favorite flowers.
An artist whose work was unknown to famous
      museums,
nevertheless had pompous theories;
he deplored the mix of paintings hung among some
      of her own
glass-framed sketches;
such cultural miscegenation, he said,
was aesthetic sin.
He had spoken with the air of a guru of all easels
and he proclaimed that her pencil work
destroyed the urgent splash and mission
of what a painter's brush-strokes
were meant to mean.
Pretending to adopt what she called his cocktail
      wisdom,

she promised, with mock piety,
to become a more careful curator
of iconographic obedience.

She was impatient to go home and re-arrange the
    future.
Showing a sudden athletic animation
that made an instant fraud of all the doctors,
it was as though there were no fatal mentions.

I could see she still loved energy
and believed that both she and I believed
that survival would obey the dictates of her will.
And so, we spoke in conjugations of another time
as though death can be tamed by grammar
or simply parsing the brutal syllables of science,
or just voicing visions.

Trapped between the image and the real,
I chatted as though a cloned ventriloquist
and diminished something of my self-esteem.

iv

She longed to go home to the brilliant palette
of her own sheets. And she asked about her
fireplace; it was guarded by sturdy andirons
and a blackened stoking piece.
She recalled a garage sale where she bought
a brass or copper vessel chased with runic symmetries
and thought to be antique. It was used for umbrellas.
And she asked after her jar of penny-wealth.
A curious concave mirror amused her
the way it gave back colors worthy
of Alighieri's flames
and the lights of passing autos in the street
always seem caught for a second-
imprisoned meteors, before they fled
into the swift instant of their flight into the dark.

I listened to her concise arrangement of time gone,
her spoken pluperfect diary.

I felt as though I walked through a labyrinth
of secret chambers in an undiscovered pyramid,
touching treasures of both then and now.

The screen before her fireplace showed a filigree
of arabesques, or perhaps scarabs and unicorns,
all caught in some stationary purpose.
I had left her favorite coffee table book open
to await her endless wonder.
It showed the baffling shapes of
a Belgian's imaginings;
it was always near the chair she used for thinking.
The double-page revealed a strange Empire of Light,
a puckish ironic of Magritte
whose dark and menacing forms always seemed to
        loiter
to devour both shadow and the suggestion of valence.
He always made miracles of water
seen through easel windows, and his stone planets
could be seen hung in space, distilling shimmer.
He bathed the world in other times
as though it were the dew of Eden.

v

She often asked that I read to her
from some Fourth Avenue treasure she had found;
fear of tigers in the night was her pretty pretense
when we read Blake together.
The broken glass of such recollections scars me
as I wander through their buttresses and walls
and try to move my tongue and voice
to sing in dry lyrics to stars
that burn in their heedless time to light our own.
It was difficult to dwell on such things,
but I did remember how she loved Blake best;
she insisted that only a good Catholic
could invent such excellence of proportion and vision
and Blake must have been a disciple of Turner,
for they both had discovered the face of God

and purified the Shangri-La of heaven's guess.
She searched for ecologies of peace
as she parsed both Blake and Turner;
she believed they must have known the
secret astonishments of Stonehenge
through their own private mysteries.

She said Blake, Turner and Magritte
were so different from those Hispanic majas
who stared from Prado walls.
Hirsute artists, she said, had stuffed their canvases
with stiff poses and haughty stares,
conquistador dandies in forced postures
of breast-plate bragging;
even their nudes were overdressed in Spanish paint.
She found offensive to her catechism
the naked bodies of Iberia,
prone dark ladies
stripped to expose suggestions of pubic sin.
The unclad myth of Genesis, she said, was different.

Such recollections whisper vain distractions;
I sit beside her bed, becoming her sullen moon
gazing down upon the doomed lover of my love.
She lies there, the warm sculpture of my doting eye
as I wish away the menace of a thousand thousand years
of broken jeopardy that gives each life
its stricken time.

She sleeps, or so it seems,
exhausted by her joy of speech,
unconscious of my pain.

Soon, a priest will come
to offer helpless comforts
of The Word in the rituals of a dead tongue,
reciting rote, a sacred mummer with
seminary advices of absolution and shriven flesh,
with miraculous medals to placate
the fallacies of pious illusion
and to sanctify the fire of flesh and the blood's heat.

He will make signs
and ready the room for the Silent Speaker,
that unknown presence who inflicts The Word
that slays rebellious life, that aborts
the instinct to resist
final meanings and strangled sounds.

The Word says rejoice
and The Word betrays the meaning of intent
and refuses to revive the happy treasons of life.

"How dark it grows," she whispers.
"I thought the sun was shining."
She believes she believes.
She smiles,
and the love that was Vesuvius in her veins
leaves a last lifted gesture
for my congress with a ghost.

Estate Nazareth
Secret Harbour
St. Thomas, Virgin Islands
Summer, 1982.

Madame, You Are Astonished

Madam, you are astonished
to behold warm lovers on this cold
bench in February;
but we are young and cannot abide
the unsure sign of touring robins.
A long war makes all life short;
do not begrudge us the flood of our small cup,
for the future is vague with neuters
and we suspect that bitter will chasten
    sweetness
into a shadow of the past.

Madam, you are old, but we are young.
You have your tidy array of archived memories
and time to browse in albums of your
    past-tense joy
and we have but now and some love,
so move on into your vault of memory;
let staid footfalls of your gentle sins
echo some by-gone revel,
some joyous indiscretion,
some timid recollection,
but we are young-
forgive us this impertinent kiss.

1942 - New York

To Be Dazzled by the Racing of Her Blood

To be dazzled by the racing of her blood,
That competition in our veins,
The loving war
That burns and heals us both
In all our fluid riddles,
Is with gods to live the legends of their birth.
Clutched and grappled,
We are shaped and joined,
Each questing for some perfect wave;
Welcomed in the rising,
The coming to impatient crest,
The plunging fall, the splashing spume,
With love astride
And roaring to a drowsing, boiling
Happiness of sweat;
And when pulsing walls in the comfort of their breach
Blaze,
The closed eyesight's palette
Dances with the innocence of original fire,
Branded with joy,
The spectrum of first flesh explodes its colors,
And there are tender frictions sledging in the easy cave,
And she who comes with me makes bright the gloom
And caresses every syllable in the syntax of all wonder.

1958 - Paris
For Yvette

Were All the Seasons Wed

Were all the seasons wed
to seldom comforts in but one discovered,
no Winter wind could scrape
and cow such matters as were once
alive with crimson temper,
bright shine of fire,
nor any phase of urgent tide of shape
offend the gleaming mood of Christmas Christ,
His jewelled Popes, His evergreens:

And you and I,
exchanging each
the comforts of our rude conditions,
can wish for better than we are,
take leave on private carousels
and go again to where we've always been.

Paris, 1960

Note:

In December, that part of the deceived world which believes it believes in Christianity, becomes an anxious host of commercial zealots and beggars (e.g., Support Our Hospitals—as though something can still be done for us), and charitable do-good cure-alls are available for all the corrugated wounds of guilt (that self-inflicted mayhem). It is a time when Goodness is bought at marked-up prices, when toy ghosts haunt the shabby house of Reality and souls (the drunken anima of us all), know, perhaps, the only redemption they will ever experience.

Remembrance is a Wintered Thing

The aspect of this winter scene,
menaced like Horatius,
lies bare and spent,
a season naked in the hills,
a season for lovers
to lie beside their gifts,
to lie beside their wishing wells
fending at their dual hells.

Note:

A feeling about the fears and elusive joys of lovers who do the best they can with what they have and who ultimately come to respect the melancholy wisdom of Ellen Glasgow after her own blunted delight and painful posture vis-a-vis her love: She lamented that love should be a passing pleasure and not a prolonged desire.

When You Have Gone From Rooms

When you have gone from rooms
Where blossoms flame in jardinieres and urns,
A scarlet hush of clustered roses settles
As though the brilliant dust of incense
Had been swallowed in a rage of unlit dooms,
And never blooming petals
And never burning suns.

Utrecht, Holland,
December, 1958.

Note:

A memoir for Yvette and for that love which makes The Emperor's New Clothing magnificently real and really perfect, as it masks the wind-breaking, bowel-moving, nose-blowing, pimples and in-grown hairs of pock-marked, limping, self-deception, after the eruptions of passion leave us dry craters of memory. But then, as Palinurus warned us, we cannot avoid our endings, unless we first avoid our beginnings.

R·I·D·D·L·E·S

Rooms sometimes need lived-in disorder,
if only for a moment;
even the imprecision of children stacking blocks
loves Pisa's crippled symmetry
and, of course, the lust for triumphant collapse.

And I, in the stumbled halt of full age,
now play infant games of haunted house,
thrusting papier-mâché bolts
to make tissue worlds secure
from thankless lovers and their serpent's teeth.

Still, to mock and defraud the truth,
I invoke awkward rituals
for undressed love
and I preen costumed and stubborn habits
to prepare our bodies,
yours and mine,
for brief conditions.

It is easier to discover secret tombs
of obscure pharaohs
or translate faded hieroglyphics
than to please love.
Frictions in their anxious tenderness
of fire and fluids
rupture on reflection and leave infected wounds;
Love's a damned elusive Pimpernel,
too polar in unseasoned weathers,
where familiar snow flakes thud and crash,
extending distances between then and now
and to where feeling finds no haven
and loses failed horizons.

Beware the good times; betray unremembered
     secrets
and avoid waiting for some expected bell,

otherwise, the door may open
showing a shredded bolt
and you will grapple alone with a smirking imp.
Keep laughter on a rigid tether
and sketch Rorschachs in what remains;
hoard some time to appease whatever,
then rush out anywhere
just after cock's crow
caressing riddles
and listening for avoided sounds.

Paris - 1988
BMcM Wright

Woodstock Revisited

Come, Christ, to our scene,
But cross on the green,
Whenever You come with Your coming;
In motley and beard,
You'll never be feared,
And traffic will chorus with humming.
Of course, we'll expect tricks
To give us our kicks,
Like walking on water un-shod;
You'll be The Blood at Woodstock,
Roll holy with rock,
Be groovy with Sly, Cream and God;
Easy Rider in joy,
Mount Zion Cowboy,
All electric with keening and wails;
Deep oceans will dry,
Fishes happily cry,
As they sing miraculous tales;
The sins of our grapples
Will sweeten green apples
And jeer at the Serpent's sharp pout;
As angels take wing,
Compete with Your Thing
And make fresh loaves of our doubt;
Amuse us, Christ Jesus,
Don't save us or tease us
As the mercies of war make us safer;
In Saigon and Hanoi,
With the death of each boy,
Engross us with wine and the wafer;
And when you have failed,
We'll have you impaled

And struck in the shape of a cross;
And as we tell to our beads
Misericordiam needs,
You'll hang like a gold albatross.

ii

Next time, come as Your Bright Bush burns,
Tell us how each gonad yearns;
Wear bell-bottom pants and dirty old sneaks,
Bring Skag and Smack and Crack for freaks,
Make us all lie down in Fields of Grass
With LSD while You say Mass;
Let every dream go up in smoke
With redolence of hash and coke;
Then amplify Your Electric Cross,
You'll be The Who, The Band, The Boss.
And as we strafe, bomb, bleed and die
And weep for doves to bless the sky,
We'll take You stoned and roll you back,
And let you brood on White and Black;
Then once again, we'll crown Your head
As You rejoin The Grateful Dead.

Note:

These Woodstock fantasies represent an excerpt from *The Hallowe'en Masques*, of Harlem's Mad Doggerelist, Lufwalnu, Nabru-Nolef, alias Brucius Dubious Africanus. It is presently out-of-print, although his *Merde in the Cathedral* is available. It has been called " ...a step in the Wright direction." Also available to those rash enough to have pipe dreams, but who wish to feel flushed with victory, is that thriller of constipation and intestinal fortitude, known as *Merde in the First Degree*. This work has been illustrated by Hieronymous Bosch.

From All The Tributaries

As in some Eden of digression
from all the tributaries
of all pain,
we can consider one another
between the footsteps of all hurry
and somehow wrestle with the closing hand
upon the capsule of our time.

Should there be no obelisk
to pierce the moment,
remember that I lay
beside your absence
like an urgent bell within an empty room;
with time hard struck upon a rapid clock,
all faith unravels like a tattered papal
    frock.

Note:

Prometheus, having attempted the felony of stealing fire from the sun, was condemned by Zeus and lashed to a rock. His liver was daily consumed by a vulture. When Chiron volunteered to suffer in the place of Prometheus, Hercules (typical of the mixed-up sexuality of the time), did combat with the vulture. How like a picture of today's various wars, rebellions, coups-d'etats and its racial torment, is the vicious legend of Prometheus. There is an American picture, too, for America remains a vast dark room in which white people develop and over-expose the negatives of black existence. The resulting image is tortured and will always be so while the camera of democracy remains so faulty.

Exhibitions

Deprived of English letters,
my true name once knew the sounds of distant places
from where dark ghosts were taken
in the captured thievery of their color
leaving them with their mark of race.
But that was a time ago.
Today, I am well clad against Christian weathers,
jungle broken;
I know the postures that imitate an alien life;
I have learned how to see Africa without nostalgia,
without tears,
without searching for the equator's shadows.
Today, I walk in vaulted hallways
where history is posed, framed and hung;
the museums give proof that primeval ancestors
once fondled stone for making fire; I am a
product of Western archaeology. Here, in this
mausoleum, for nominal admission,
one can practice superior staring and feel evolved.
In the wonder of Cretan caves, Thracian graffiti
and wild creatures walking upright.
I can marvel at my dark image as I pause,
place an elbow on a marble mantel
and I gaze upon the produce
of learned excavations.

On any Sunday, I can visit Africa in New York,
skim backward over the Middle Passage
and view an aborted home through the frame
of some electric-lighted tomb
for lost and unremembered worlds, integrated, too,
for the crumbled wonders that once were Golden
    Greece
and Caesar's Rome. Both are immigrants here;
here they all are, the one-time tenants

of Olympus and the Seven Hills,
captured and transported like my ancient African
    fathers.
These cold artifacts, these icon remnants
somehow seem more welcome in this pale world
than the color-wheel progeny of ante-bellum commerce.
Still, these bothersome infants of time
seem well dressed in impeccable Sabbath suits.
but they speak in tongues unpronounced in Yoruba.
Now and then, as I turn my head,
I become a Homer contemplating the false face
reflected in an ancient mirror;
I trespass among the swaddles of Egyptian dead
that show the wrappings and unwrappings of
Rosetta's Stones.
The arctic speech of English
bites through time, profanes the classical ecology
of curiosity about my former time and place.
My evolution winces in alarm—
I wonder if I am where I am.
Diverted, I steal a look at my sturdy crease;
I must not attract a critical look;
I touch my lapel, trace its shape
(a far weep from the crude pubic covers
shown in the peep-show National Geographic candor);
I note the bold announcement of my black taste,
its spun cloth and the glossed coverings of my feet.
How came I among such carefully clad throngs,
these upright moving figurines?
The stitched design of my trappings,
buttoned and zippered into crafted style,
clothe and camouflage
my mutant siblings of the lost bloodlines;
we are a pride of eunuch lions waltzing
and well shod; our theology of manners
paints black Tarzans savaged from the Niger's
dark distances by traders of my nude beginnings
and Christian endings. I dream of
braided patterns and amulets that tremble and tinkle

39

with their burden of burnished trifles—
artful Benin garnish hanging an artful canon,
golden totems . . .
I envision dark ladies in their royal time,
their hair a formal garden of precise rows
as they march, shimmering models,
mannequins come to life for every Adam.
I breathe fire into their veins,
these black graces
of my reverie, proud in their sheen;
and now, they are exiles to frozen latitudes
seducing cold geography, suggesting Shango visions.
I wonder if pale haughtiness delights,
gazing upon these clones of captured cultures.
They walk, endowed with surpassing scorn,
each one a sovereign, mocking common needs.
In this hall of displaced pillage,
the quarried thefts from Carrara, too,
remind the memory of famous dates and places,
the grand patrons who endowed easels, the sculptors
who dared produce the face of God
or sculpt the wooden angels for the ships of slavers
and glaze the surgery of the Sacred Heart,
heaven's judgments, papal walls;
but suddenly, the black condition intrudes
upon bleached history; touching time,
it passes behind shadowed epochs preceding Eden,
then wears the beard of Moses
or perhaps an Easter Island face.
The symmetry of darkness has become a rage of devils
struggling with a dance of angels amazing grace.
The adopted faith and transfused blood
of long-dead patriarchs
are made both seminal and rash,
loudly pentecostal in treason to forgotten tribal vows.
ii
Briefly, the face of a red displaced chief
was found engraved upon a copper coin,
while bleached guilt is engraved upon the shining land

40

that sings hymns as the tricks of bondage refuse to flee.
And now, the once-before bondsmen
have pledged their lives and deaths
to pale pieties,
professing in their captured diaspora.
The syllables of England's stepmother tongue
now command dark imported fate.
What a surprise, if ancestors in their
melanin imprisonment
could behold well-clad figures in their
crazy quilt of permutations
in the whole cloth of America's unwashed quirks
that have arraigned us all in English names.

We speak in Celtic syllables
and now and then focus on the lost lands
of Africa; or our exiled Carib stares
give loving looks towards Whitehall's London
where Azikewes and Cudjoes have changed their
          manners.
Eurocentric in our images,
we mimic Mayfair's contemplations;
our indelible dilutions
in their miscellaneous rage of genes
have made poets of the once colonies
pursue La Négritude, the bewitched goddess,
as they translate Afroisms into
the politesse of French;
Senghor, Damas, Césaire, leave unspoken
the ancient gutterals of their unmixed fathers
and prosper in the metaphors of Diderot and Voltaire,
as Naipal curses Trinidad and India.

Alas, for poor La Négritude,
the once and still literary ghost,
as its authors hope that all they have to say
will somehow define their égalité.

For false faces everywhere
All Saints Eve, Paris, 1965.
BMcMW

41

Homage to the Virgins

I. With Vague Strangers Descending.

Cushioned upon this polished altitude
With vague strangers descending,
Our jets are calmed and we praise their powered hush
    and roar;
The navigator's calculus made true,
A compass yields a rising of geography:
There, floating, lies an island
Framed in its dark green focus.
The slow ellipse of our wings tilts the planet;
Deranged, the sun is everywhere.
From our distance, the mampoo trees, sprung from lava,
    stand still
Where neither springs nor rivers slake their roots;
Above that crawling nature of a hundred million deaths
    in hiding,
We cannot yet see the Bouganvillaea bleed
Among the vines and secrets lick out at moving shadows
And life's blind murders creep in their thousands.

With engines digesting air, our pilot prepares
His electric panel for a scientific swoop upon the
    ocean garden;
The black geometry of our profile
Is thrown down upon the windward waters;
It races for a moment on the surface of the painted sea,
Speeds its vanished tracings over each coral prism,
Then leaps its contours upon the land
And turns with us again,
Until we hang,
Almost still.

Insistent patterns push up from below
And crumbled history shows its ruined pulse;
The smell of time is almost seen as we glide closer;
Strangled piles suggest dead sugar mills

And speak of immigrants from Elsinore,
Telling of gray phantoms from a Danish dream
Of kidnapped tribes, rich fields of sweet cane,
Magas, brick ovens, copper coils
And then the rum which warmed the northern taste of
    Scandinavia.

Wounding the hills, lost roads scratch away at instant growth
And beaches move their figures slowly
As though naked chessmen wakening to life.
Our noisy hover moves over Mermaid's Chair, near
    Sandy Bay;
The burning palette breathes and
We see a painting come to life:
Emancipated now, black first consuls
And tribunes of these sea-thrown hills,
Fulanis, Ibos, Kalibaris,
Multiply their English-speaking gift of tongues;
The ocean blood of Africa laps at secret harbours
Named Bolongo, Sunsi, Tutu, Cowpet and Perseverance;
In a green remembrance of another sun,
Tiny jungles mystify clouded mountain heights
Embracing all the tenses man has engrafted onto time.
Even now, an arid cumulus of promise hangs reluctant
Over this bright scene,
A miser in the refusal of its gift of flood.
It was always so from the beginning,
When hungry Caribs must once have danced for rain
In the hard vocation of their need,
For they owned the slopes where sculptured condominiums
And modern legends of Bluebeard now make expensive
    trespass.
                        ii
Just off the piers, where peculiar traffic
Once swallowed up a Christian conscience,
There remains a one-time market for the flesh of all
My fathers;
Now the merchants of well plucked foods and other
    creatures.
The abrupt land plunges upward from the water,

Hiding the distance and its dissecting stony trails;
Shadowed surfaces appear
As though harried by some heedless glacier from a
    foreign pole;
A grudge of wild growth invites some doubtful cows
Moving with the melancholy stumble of desert beasts,
Sparse in body, pinched in bone.

But, addicted by the dazzle of the sun, beauty has no beasts;
When daytime rises to my fallow need,
I am no longer a student of this magic place,
Nor is it proper to brood overlong upon some
Spent and ancient time
When Christian piety trapped my race
To dwell on bitter and cultivate harsh fields of sweet.

II. *The Functions of the Sky.*

How I loved and hated the functions of the sky,
Its blinding nativity of light,
All rape and wrestle in my hot waterfall
Of sweat and doze;
I lie upon the earth, as though rooted to the shore,
At my own mercy of sloth and lost temper, gazing
at the slow-motioned tide foaming
In mock anger, then sliding down the ramp of beach;
I burn to take my shadow
To some shade and touch its shifting mercy,
But I only stare, measuring the light in its millimeter
Of stealthy movement
In the sun's constant celebration.

The world has fled;
Only swift-plunging Orions preying upon the sea
Can splash time a little
And let me know how near I am to murder
As fish-hawks and pelicans dive avid
At their victims off the Coki shallows.
My siesta seems endless in its shimmer;
It was here, perhaps, that Columbus knelt
And pledged the patronage of St. Thomas to this place.

In other centuries, the once-green jungles
Were never slashed by urban paths;
But once upon an ancient time, not even the Old World's
Infallible pretensions of the popes
Could match these burning waters, the rainbows of
their depths.

My respiration almost ceases; the sand becomes glass dreams
In my urgeless metaphysics;
An indolence of wind ignores the braising of my flesh
And, in a storm of visions, I store up life forever;
Dante's vocation leaps alive. He must have known
The special burning of this sun
To write his searing mark upon the world;
I feel as one with his sentence to life, his ordered death
By fire, the exile of his disdain,
As I count the winnings of my paradise found,
The blindness of my ex-communication from all that I
    have fled:
Beggars for time, Alighieri and I
Have nursed upon the bread of strangers.

I wake to watch a brilliant flash of birds
In Biblical bushes,
As they dart in their shrill imperative;
I see a panting dog, dripping its tongue
With what man is pleased to believe is a smile.
It moves along the boiling surf,
Leaving perfect footprints to be swallowed by the tide;
Like a four-legged Aphrodite, it has stepped from the
    wet brine
To shake off a mist of sun-trapped colors;
It could be the Second Coming, for all I know,
An almost water-walking Advent.

The time is glad with light
And rude fountains continue to boil and bubble in my flesh;
Then suddenly, as though a blacksmith drowns his burning
    metal,
The day is gone.
The sun becomes a fevered parallactic shape,

45

And then it has fled.
It is the only swiftness in these tropics,
Except when rain strikes with its wet whip from the hills,
And then, water floods the talk of these islands
    floating arid,
And the green thirst of mountains and roof-top pipes
Drink weather to be hoarded from the plumbing.

While water rages from above,
That is the time to weep
And think upon the losses of this El Dorado.

Counting mysteries
In a children's hour of days,
I give hard study to the Rorschachs in the clouds,
Seeking out in the *cumulus humilis*
The faces in God's painted sky.

Early to the beach, as day is born again,
I worship with a congregation of winter pilgrims
In their religion of light,
While frozen cities in their far remove
Brittle against their chap and phlegm.
And when I have counted out the reduction of my days,
I will return to my chilled tensions
And through the customs declare my black boast of sun,
As though an overdose of purification by fire
Can cure the world of its sorrow over darkness.

In ways I seldom say, I love such lone days
Of counting waves and other repetitions;
In the mathematics of an idle total, I have
Watched the ocean move in virtue to its tides;
I have gazed upon a carnival and reached for its hidden joys
Behind the false face of exaggerated life;
I have flung my functions all upon the ground,
There to be kindled in the sun
And melting there, I have brooded upon Shelley's death
And the drinking of his Mediterranean flood;
His heart, fallen into his funeral flames, refused to burn
Upon his last Italian shore. I thought, too,

Of Proust and Joyce,
And of their famous reputations
For focusing on remote detail to embalm each
    recollection.
I was licensed to engage
All visions never dared before,
With drowning near enough to touch.

Now and then, I lifted up mine eyes unto the hills
Where the blessed poor, condemned to their meager huddle,
Inherit the earth
And dwell in the shadow of the prickly bush.

The tide glistens
And the bathers come. They speak of scuba and coral;
Some flourish in the shallows;
Others, masked in goggles, false gills sand rubber flippers,
Move like a prehistoric legend,
Break the tinted surface
And submerge as Peeping Toms to gaze at naked fishes.

I lie in wait for Eve,
And I am Adam.

Recollections of time passing
and of the sea and sand,
sights, scenes and smells sur-
rendering to sloth at Coki
Point, Saint Thomas, Virgin
Islands, beyond the siege of
winter [but not creditors.]

Circa 1973.

Tar Babies

When I was a child and discovered my skin
and learned that black is the color of sin,
I wept nightmares that flooded my head
(my father thought I had wet in my bed);
sometimes my dreams were menaced by giants
more awful than monsters out of frightening science;
they had bleeding eyes and ebony fangs—
no warlock could have caused more shivery pangs.

In school, I was taught about the fairy tales
and learned that ogres were dark and fearsome males,
swarthy, blacker than any dread-filled night,
teeming with slimey shapes of fright,
flaming devils, demons, gargoyled elves
all multiplied by tens and twelves.
Tar Babies, I was taught, were delinquent, immoral,
wicked, evil, ominous in each bitter quarrel;
I wondered how Little Black Sambo could smile
or make his darkness reconcile
his circumstance with Snow White's life-
he was, I thought, a symbol of strife.

I advanced through classes and into high school
where I sometimes felt like a slandered fool;
I read Dubose Heyward, Joseph Conrad, Mark Twain
and I was told there was no reason for me to complain;
The Nigger of the Narcissus, my teacher explained,
was not anti-Negro (she could see I was pained),
and had nothing to do with race, color or hue,
but I could discover not one other clue
to parse the Korzeniowsky theme,
nor did that Pole comfort one single dream.
The Dubose Heywards, of course, were experts on blacks,
they knew plantation darkies and all ethnic facts;

they invented *Mamba's Daughters* and *Porgy and Bess*
and gave smirking catfish gleeful access
to midnight fears well-mixed with horror:
I feared that the world would revoke each tomorrow.

I hated such authors, their every cold device
such as Uncle Tom and Eliza eloping on ice;
blemished idylls spun by Mark Twain,
I saw his heroes as grim and profane;
Huckleberry Finn, Tom Sawyer, each in his way,
remain white heroes, even today,
but poor black Jim becomes an ingrate in his flight
from Christian bondage and Caucasian spite:
He was devastated by Mark Twain's craft,
symbolically, upon a raft.

I grew to hate *The Emperor Jones*,
Devil's Food Cake and chocolate cones;
no enlightened wisdom could quite demolish
my detestation for black shoe polish;
but I fumed as Al Jolson with his burnt-cork face
got rich stealing Mammy from my race;
Bre'er Rabbit, Uncle Remus, Amos 'n Andy
pretended that black is happily fine and dandy
and they made their lies a national cause,
sanctifying white mental pause.

In France, my friends are betrothed to their mousse,
but no taste bud's treason could ever induce
my appetite to traduce its vow
to hate all chocolate both then and now;
and yet, the women to whom I've been wed
and sought to please in life and bed,
have been Dark Ladies in their grace,
moreso than in Will Shakespeare's case.

Now that I'm old and quasi-reconciled
with the obscenities that life has filed,

I understand each Moor's genetic aphorism
that allows me to gaze upon every racial prism
and see that life can be distilled from what is black
and I laugh at the lies about all that I lack,
although internally, I sometimes scream a quest
to discover that Black is Beautiful and Best,
but I know the feeling when dark gonads yearn
for what society says their love must spurn
and I know black men weep when mandates of the heart
are overruled before they start:
Recall brave Othello's jealous curse
that placed false Iago's treason first
and given his darkly troubled choice,
the demented Moor murdered Desdemona's voice.

At a United Nations Cocktail Party

Thoughts at a formal cocktail party at the United Nations, where formerly colonized victims of imperialism and the rape of Africa, played hosts to their former captors and regaled them by speaking the languages of the conquerors, aping their manners and smiling incessantly in gracious too-muchness. The Africans act as though it has always been the best of all possible lives in the best of all possible worlds, with no trespassers on the face of Mother Africa. Thus, a well-mannered scene becomes obscene.

In hand-crafted and tailored suits,
The Africans have chopped away their roots;
Impeccable, each tropic pro-consul stands,
Each says, for the independence of their lands;
But conquerors still hold hypnotic sway
Over what Blacks do and how they say.

Equatorial dialects and tongues
Do not betray dark mouths or lungs;
Shod and preened men hold cigarettes with ease,
They smile and bow and seek to please;
Their women, swathed in brilliant silk and kente,
Now tell their chefs to cook *al dente*.
Not missionaries now, of course,
Although there may be retroactive remorse.

Each Delegate who precisely speaks,
Makes one wonder what each one seeks;
They make no mention, small or grand,
In language from their motherland,
The accents are Oxford, Cambridge, or Gaul's
At all receptions, debates or balls;
A European idiom defines their arts
And appears to have won their minds and
    hearts;
They ignore their tribal dialects

They baffle history, betray their race
And this tells us something of their place.

The northern thieves who conquered them,
Who looted their mines of ore and gem,
Who called them nigger, kafir and worse,
Then gave them freedom and an empty purse,
Must smile as they see what they have done
And realize what has been lost and what
        was won.
All those customs, once endeared,
Have all but died and disappeared;
Now Afro-Saxons in their ways and dress,
They've learned to pray and how to bless;
Their animistic gods are dead,
Now Jesus troubles in each head,
With the Rosary exchanged for worry beads.

Missionaries need no longer fear
That they'll be cooked and disappear;
Where once stood totems, proud and tall,
Transmogrified natives now heed the call
Of Canterbury or a nuncio from Rome:
They all seem lost, so far from home.

White shadows stain each dark cause
With remnants of the conqueror's laws;
Urbane, dainty and most polite,
Their past seems buried and out-of-sight;
Jungle potions are no longer poured
And ancient folkways are now ignored;
In the villages where they were born,
Witch Doctors merit only scorn;
They hear priests and rectors proudly boast
Of God's salvation through the Holy Ghost,
And now, with incense, hymns and Psalter,
Black converts kneel before an altar
Upon rich carpets, red as blood,
Instead of dust or village mud;
In postures of the pious humble,

They give communion their zealous mumble;
Mannered elegance is what they know
And their costly tailors from Saville Row.
                    II
When Third World diplomats convene,
They show how they can be obscene;
High fashion and hypocrisy merge
In suppressing what should be their urge;
Beau Monde politesse is all the rule
In the scandals of this false-faced school.

Blacks smile at whites who stole their wealth
And drink martinis to their health:
How shall I tell the world that's Third
That it and the First are both absurd?

Note:

In 1982, the Nigerian ambassador to the United Nations convened a cocktail party in the Delegates Lounge of the ethnic mélange of miscellaneous genes on Manhattan's East River. Although I remain an urban peasant, I somehow received an engraved invitation, probably because of my friendship with Léopold Sédar Senghor, who always introduced me as a "well known black American poet." The natives were dressed in the formal habits of their former rulers, as they imitated life at the top, pranced pretentiously in the presence of their European masters and generally struck impressive poses.

As I regarded these dark and stylish clones of their former oppressors and wondered about their semi-emancipation, I recalled a racist *TARZAN* film I once saw two of my very young sons watching. It was called *TARZAN IN NEW YORK*. One sequence showed Tarzan, awkwardly and uncomfortably clad in a suit and hat walking along Park Avenue. His attention was drawn to the figure of a black doorman. Tarzan, feigning amazement, pointed to the man and exclaimed, "Ha, they put clothes on him, too!"

E. T., wherefore art thou?

Bruce Wright, a/k/a
Lufwalnu Nabru-Orgen.

"Many more people than do
might commit suicide, except
for their fear of what the
neighbors might say."

-Palinurus.

A Grace of Ghosts

As clean as bleached white bone,
My book shelves mock at fear of life
With testaments of hastened death.
Huddled near at hand and brain,
A grace of ghosts
Stands trapped in coats of many colors;
They dance their syllables in a petrified dirge
In their bright wrapping-paper shrouds.
Sung to by print, they are wrapped in winding sheets
Of parchment, wimpled now,
For Jerrell, Plath, Sexton, Berryman, Hemingway,
All lost within the echo and the maze of
Bangs and whimpers.

They acted out their final metaphor
And set murder at each stricken image;
I have elected to wait.
They were impatient for Godot
And they fled from all their anxious causes
Towards the dead-end of their consequence,
The forever toll of Samara.
Racing deep into the mouth of greedy questions,
They could have lingered in our bluster
To wait for time to assassinate all our blood discomforts,
For time is a temperament of spite,
A villain in the marrow and the veins,
A rush for baffled epitaphs
In sullen praise of rituals and buried clay,
A doubtful hunger for the passion of the earth,
Where the hue and courtesy of undertakers
Mocks the jurors of our last complaint.

Christina Leit-Motifs

Gaze upon the mystery of the moving sea
Close to how the drowning edge
Slakes at dry discords rejected by the tide;
Watch it as it sinks into the shore and swallows itself again
As though digesting all piety and every depth.

Dear Christina, you who made first fluids
Make a mocking noise
Bursting swollen veins in the lava of their flood,
You have taken harsh grace and instruction from the skies
And bathed by guilt, you first ignite, then snuff out
That sudden flame where blood and marrow boil;
You have allowed white shapes clad in black habits
To speak lections and flog your secret quarrels,
And, like those pale nuns of God,

You have suppressed glad frictions
Troubling in your thighs;
And so ministered,
You are not tempted into defiance of God's women
Who fondle vows and mute morals;
Nor will you be defiled
Or wrestled by some hissing serpent in its coils;
I see you in the distance of a forbidden mirror
As you dance gratified upon the needle in my flesh;
Unclean in my hot eruption,
I listen to your mouthed hosannas to piety and arid lies.

ii

Dear Christina, with your syllables of Christ,
Romanize and make civil this savage Moor,
Grant indulgences, light candles, put fire to some holy wick
To warm us both unto some amazing shore;
Then will I stand, wounded by passion.
Confessed and unshriven,
I have been an aspen to the sudden symmetries upon your face

And you, who have raced my visions through each
    forbidden door
To Carthage, where Desdemona never dared,
Will find in me a ruder Samson, captured, wept and shorn,
Unworthy to be consecrated in your place,
For Methusela's ghost-years haunt my search for that grace
Of Thisbe, Troilus and dead loves of long ago.
I hear that Sirens still sing somewhere translations
Of their endless choir,
And have even strayed quick comets from their hastened way,
Even as I speed no closer in my ancient chase
To where your springtime
Declines to resurrect what all my instincts say.
I am left to watch green dolphins writing children's books,
And turning pages of un-titled tales.

iii

Where actuaries gamble in their games with death
And wager on its rude decisions,
They convene with rituals of time to caress life's harshest
Moment
With a serpentine angle aimed upon a graph,
Precisely geared to fall upon an ultimate prediction;
The premium thus fixed,
Measures out an undertaker's lien,
Beyond redemption of what life was insured against.
Policies justify their cold calculus
Before the paint of portraits glazes in formaldehyde.
Then, with the corpse made pretty for Jesus
And His resurrections,
A priest will preside
Whose creed of conscience confesses that he never really knew
The secret sweat of sinful clay.
But he re-shapes the body and the fled soul
Like a potter correcting fractured form
And he speaks of God among the sweetened chemicals of faith,
Compelling his sacred arithmetic of beads,
Exacting a Latin phrase or two,

Pronouncing an obligatory, un-rhymed verse;
He will then move his lips
In a song that bites the mouth
With sorrow and grovels in the earth
With praises which fail to move the subject
Of his pious taxidermy
And latter-day Egyptian art:

And where the calculated line has not yet plunged,
Ancient kinsmen of the ape chorus a wake
And serenade their sacred totems.

iv

When our ghosts are preened and holy,
Prepared to rise and flee to satin tombs,
The far ecology of heaven will no longer deny our coming;
Angels, it is said, may sing a *missa solemnis* tuned to Bach,
And although such music triumphs over
The dry dirges of Wesley for those slain by death,
The young, who die in their surprise,
Prefer the better balance
Of guru lyrics sung by Eleanor Rigby to her Beatles,
Or even the well-tempered Grateful Dead.

One day, perhaps, our stark hymnals will discover
How to salvage joy and recollect the glad faults of living,
When disposing of life;
And then, a jig of glee can seize
Gloomy bearers of our pall
As they shout a black requiem to match a strut on
Bourbon Street, recalling how little David
Once danced before the Lord with all his might.

v

The living must remember a passion in the touch
Of breathing flesh,
All those throbbing spurts of life
Denied to common priest and pope alike,
When man's true coming
Bore naked witness

To a gift of pubic bushes burning in the beauty
Of flaming sweat,
When love, consumed, screamed and re-wrote Genesis.
It was then that God, who invented Eve,
Must have smiled
And been greedy for the taste of love's fevered waters.

vi

When sight deceives the drunk imaginings of love,
One thinks that there is always too much distance
Dividing nights and days;
But when prisms shatter into separate colors,
One then perceives the poses,
The postures, trapped as though in granite.
It was then, I saw you,
Even as Adam must have grown to weep for Eve,
And she for him;
You were always in bondage to distances of your own,
Indentured to a harsher law,
Wrestled by some testament of statutory passion.

There was never any index to our loss, and no need;
Nothing was discovered to bend our parallels to meet;
Our different chapters had no common meaning
Although it seemed the same calendar
Marked identities which darkened
How the Zodiac had confused our sighs.
Alas, poor Adam,
He, too, must have wondered how to know
What seasons he should fear,
Or how to seize and purify with Eve—
A woman with no jewels or red enamel for her nails,
And only a natural parting in her hair;
A woman, nevertheless, although bereft of knowing
Any of The Twelve Signs and their symbology.

Dear Christina, you are caught between the Virgin and
     Scorpio,
For you are Libra, balanced in a lifetime diary
Of your borrowings from duration,

While all the burning years escape.
We cannot long indenture time,
Nor have you learned from your studies
And old common laws
That when time is past, there is no pastime.
And so, imprisoned in my losses,
I leave you to your Italian graces, your papal candles
And the crossed scar from your Roman inoculation.
You will learn that time comforts the dead,
While undertakers of our passion, those pale priests
And nuns in their haunted black parade,
Hunger to devour our sins
And prescribe parables and therapeutic words
To drown our fluids,
Transmuting that glory into cold bubbles from the pores.
And in the coming nights,
You and I will never hear the beauty of hard breathing
From the other.

Estate Nazareth, St. Thomas,
Virgin Islands,
1977.

Moon Walks

Why go to the moon to dance in its dust
Disturbing the dirt in its serrated rilles?
The image of craters and dehydrated lakes
Have conspired to steal the lunatic lust
Of what we regarded as our Valentine totem;
But now, stripped bare by Kodak's hard focus,
We see that the moon is a spatial hag,
Barren of seminal juices, cold lava,
Its heights, its steeples,
Its uneven teeth,
Its rootless canals,
Its stony acne,
Its grotesque wrinkles,
Defy the loving Hallmark pentameter,
Our crimson ribbons and hearts of a season
Are lost in the dry swirls
And rough needles of petrified shale.

How did this litter, this rude harshness
Make pregnant the verse of
Lovelace, Shelley, Keats?
The masked and camouflaged men who
    sampled its surface,
Who hung weightless,
Who gallowed our fictions,
Can never again stare up at the moon,
See its bright rising,
Its symmetries of shine,
And grasp for a quill,
Foolscap and thought,
Or be blinded by their eyes
And what they behold.

ii

We, who have never probed distant orbits,
Can rejoice in the fraud of our satellite

And wonder how fortune and its seers of signs
Have the divisible gall to endow planets
    with sense,
With sexual suggestion
Or forecasts of Kismet
With warnings, cautions
And alarums of fate.
Has the zodiac betrayed its omens,
Leaving the crisp crescent of cookies
To conceal some sly Szechuan prank?

And yet, how wonderful it was when
Innocence could love the lies
Told by poets,
Those symbolist soothsayers
Who gave us such moonstruck
Syllables for sympathetic parsing,
Giving great distances to our drama and
our dreams.

Ah, yes, the moon, that once and affectionate
    icon,
Nailed like a picture on the wall of space,
Commanding the menstrual tides of our seas,
Defining its fullness, its halves, its quarters,
Its invisible side,
Sharing its false light,
Its imagined smile.

It was our visible God out there in the heavens;
We submitted to its far hypnosis,
Its concealed and counterfeit fire,
Allowing us to be caught
Upon its cusp of deceit.

Berkeley, California On
A Commencement Occasion,
And While Flying Over The
Barrens of the Sierra Nevadas.
25 May, 1992

In Guard We Trust

We stand guard at
poisoned wishing wells
beneath a palisade of news reports;
now and then we pretend at glee
but sing sad songs
like Auld Lang Syne.
As midnights get struck
in artificial zones of time,
we often kiss assassins,
help them hone their blades
and wish Happy New Year
to vague strangers in the dark.

Midnight moments can sedate
the fears of bristling gloom,
anesthetize miscarried
meditations that
assault imprisoned entrances
to our private hells;
the face of time's false delight
smiles upon each newest year;
beware that rouged rogue
dressed in spangles and a pointed hat,
wearing a smirking mask
and all its merry grammar
dancing through its fretful lark.

We beam resolves upon this seasonal mimic
camouflaged in bright mascara,
this witling of mischief,
this shadow creature,
this youthful morning-after gargoyle,
this dentured carnivore,
greedy for us all.
Be cautious in your merriment;
the year becomes a vicious clown

in Joseph's coat
of swarming patterns
that will baffle the zodiac's metaphors
and blind the insolent vision of seers.

When distances and seasons come closer
and this buffoon night
is ghosted and daggered in our ruins,
we can wonder how
our drenched dreams of incest
have been ambushed into tiny shatters.
And when the next December ends,
we will marvel that our marvelous minds
can peer into houses with no windows,
cut recollections in chiseled stone,
the cold luminous of granite,
when, once again,
a New Year looms and leers.

By Brood McM. Wright, a/k/a
Bruise McM.
Brute McM., etc.
Circa 1994.

Cadro, Switzerland

This risen village has been swept and rinsed
for three hundred years. Italy lies hidden
behind snow-tops to the south. One elder,
claiming he helped make the past, points to
where Hannibal hiked his herd of elephants.
Fire and water define the dawn as creation rises
from the steaming drapery of mist. Unnoticed
on any travel agent's map, mornings are stealth and
    wisp.

My terrace looks away from the sun's first light;
minor Alps pose in God's bright gleam; His strobe,
or Her's. Lake Lugano, trapped between rude rocks,
is a pane of rippled glass,
a zig-zag shape from heaven's crazy quilt.
The Caesars, on their march to Gaul left
this hillside silence behind; But a Roman mark,
makes its accent here and speaking is all gestures
and oral passion.
The houses confess a lover's craft
Their chimneys flatter soot in their delicate
craftsmanship of doll house temples
attended by laughing angels sculptured
to their roof-top duty.

1601, says a dated arch. It looks it,
chipped but sturdy in the mountain weather.
The cemetery is older, and so is death,
but not as old as life.

St. Rocco is the patron saint of this hidden place;
His church is draped in blood red;
Scarlet candles warm his adoration
and he is remembered by those who never knew him;
Father Boconfuso, proud of his English limitations,
recalls Rocco's miracles and touches
the fresh flowers at Rocco's concrete feet.

The parish is poor; there are no marble images.
A clock tower tolls the hourly deaths of time
marking merciless minutes measuring failed meaning;
Purpose passes, and a writer sits, waiting to welcome
sought bondage to The Word;
a leering surface of empty paper
dares a suitable scribble, a revised revision,
an altered change, an after-thought,
an interlineation, deletion, modification,
scratch-out, restoration, a truthful fiction,
a wrong assessment, a cryptic phrase, a forgotten secret
and confessions to a priest of paper.

The bell rings another arid hour; I may
as well write messages to dead strangers. Something.
Strangers, the divorced professor says,
are better to love. Their rights-of-way
allow them to touch and cross like shadows
with no time to weep for a second clutched entangle
or scandalous kisses.
Strangers in their awkward and cold commerce,
their Rubick's cube of groping limbs,
have no time for seminal dissatisfactions
and no wish to overcome or challenge
what might have been.

Here, in this lost village with unwritten words,
one can dream of Pied Pipers piercing mountains
to divert the blame of who and why and when—
and send it elsewhere. In far places inside,
there may be no light; but here, it is dawn.

Cadro, Switzerland,
overlooking Lugano
Summer - 1986.

Gallileo's Dark Sahara

Pressing round the lava shape of earth
Are frozen ocean spaces.
Out temperate meteor,
Arrested in the petrified circle of its limits,
Hangs like a clouded picture upon the air;
It is there,
Whirling in its invisible spin,
Losing its daily race with the sun,
It hangs;
A stolid, harsh balloon,
Buffeted by the turbulence of first cause,
It hangs,
Obedient to its place;
Mated to a cold lover,
It yields its tides to the dead bauble of a moon.

Merlins, dissecting secrecy,
Make studious mumble
In Greek and Latin on their stellar maps;
Planets receive arrogant definitions,
Mercator's flat mistakes are humbled
And cold craters are christened anew
As speculators probe the fires of geology
That light our years;
They send the chauffeurs of their science
To invade the distance;
Awkward angels, dressed in immunized
    precautions,
They are aliens
To the cherubs of Christ or Michaelangelo:
And now, we know the neighborhood
Of Galileo's gazed upon lofty dark Sahara.

ii

Within our menaced membrane,
We cling to temper and the mystery of breath;
And those who reject the holy science of Genesis,
Are magnetized to the Magis' stars;

They preach a passion of obeisance
To the arithmetic of feeling;
They believe they believe
And that Trinity is both three and one;
But the guru argonauts of space
Prefer a gospel according to Einstein;
They take communion with relativities,
They relish the bite of Newton's apple
And they rejoice in the sin of knowing.
Nobel wisdom dares desert bleakness
Of places beyond lost air;
And then, in tongues and codes,
They speak of heaven's fires
And let us brood on Satan's vengeful arson.

iii

The blinding mystery of the sun
Makes us fondle falsehoods
And we believe that the moon shines.
In the poetry of fortune tellers,
Accountants of the sky's laboratory litter
Dot their charts with Dippers, a belted hunter
And, for the faithful, an altar and an ark.
But, in the big bang realm of quiet,
Without marked time or fickle season,
The stoic moon perseveres, a failed Icarus;
It seems fastened there,
A Pavlov's dog of orbit.

The scholars of its dirt tell us how it is
Entombed in the pulver of its drowned dead seas;
It is, some writings say,
A spatial mummy,
An aloof and spectral lover of the earth,
A mute whimper of its ancient noise.
And yet, more than a gelded ball,
More than a black lamp,
It has kindled seminal images;
Deaf and dumb, it reflects the sources
Of music, blood and heat in its neuter mirror;
Its vacant pulse lured Lear to madness,
Flooded Bluebeard's uxorial abattoir,
Made crimson the ashes of Holocaust,

Drove Christians in their pious felonies
Of geography,
Their larcenous ethic of black bondage,
And it watched nude Africans
Adopt their owners' genuflect.

Ah, yes, the moon;
Glued upon our minds,
It remains a relic in the air,
A still-life in its dry and dusty drama;
It is a lightless wick,
A thief of glimmer.
Reflecting false faces,
Its cold crust has made mankind inflame itself,
Sing songs and celebrate painful postures
In a madness named as love.
But there is no man in the moon,
And no woman,
Except those now-and-then trespassers
In their hermetic camouflage
Who dance like puppet ghosts
And seem to float upon the dust they agitate;
Athletic robots,
They rob our rituals of their fluids,
Topple pentecostal steeples
And jeer the seven-day Jehovah germinal.

Out there, in that vast hole,
Gods and devils can be lost in back of space;
And once the stars are reduced
To formulae, an axiom, an infallible
Calculus of man's rivalry with the Sire of Jesus,
Where, then, shall a seeker of visions look?

Night Visions and Moon
Thoughts On The Beach,
Grande Case, Saint Martin,
French West Indies And
Anguilla, British West Indies,
circa January 2nd, et seq.,
1985.

B. Wright, Who Would
Rather B. President.

68

V·I·R·G·I·N·A·L·S

Imprisoned behind trellis bars
a fern springs from a painted pot;
sea shells plant green avocados,
a conch is fertile in its promise
of tart and tiny lemon trees from Araby;
loving signs in Gothic print are Baedekers
of a Latinate geography
ignoring English synonyms
with syllables that tax the tongue's idiom.

Dressed in widow's black,
the farmer of this ordered jungle window-shelf
prefers the language of a Roman past
for the progeny of her humus, her induced
      miscegenation
that sheds ovarian grace
upon her hybrid wedding seeds—
not the intimate seed of a different bed,
of course,
for, as with nuns, those neuter sisters of the flesh,
she has saved her ultimates
in the way that misers of the never-spent
do counting out, caressing things.

The problems of her paradox are epidemic:
She makes obeisance to the stern canon law,
dressing miniature holy ghosts in the way that
pre-pubic mothers pamper plastic dolls;
and then, there is the law of a distant sky
making ivy climb to her otherwise forbidden
      entrances,
for she knows her seed and the genius of how
it becomes a fern
and she hints at secrets in the plain and prim
slang of her husbandry,
and she blushes often when tipping the gushing
      phallus
of her watering vessel;
it is then she becomes a red and wet leaf

from Eden's plucked tree,
creating crises of botanical shame;
on such occasions
she longs for sanctuary behind
fig leaves of Smyrna
to cover baffled needs
in those moments when she must abort lust;
she knows the word *fern* is but a poor alias invoked
to mask the seminal definition of *polypodium
    verginianum;*
sometimes, she simply sits and beholds her
    vegetation,
but then, her visions are too often raped
by a leafy prurience; in mute conversation
and pleading, she tries to
traduce the arrogance of each naked trespass
gleaned from the daily drama of her breedings
that fertilize and reproduce on the altar of her
window sill.

The brazen ivy seeking to make wrongful entry
in its green and serpentine ambition, is *hedera helix;*
its Icarus complex pays strict allegiance
to its heaven of blazing sun;
she must prune its wild rampage.

In her dark black habit, she will often
stare at her conch;
it is her arid and strangely barren horn of plenty
(*strombus alatus*), seductive in its hollowed grace,
sensual in its temptation of fondles
for its smooth concave evisceration
and, like God, a symbol of loneliness,
Then branded below where her rosary hangs,
she knows she is rebuked by God's indignation;
such arousals must be exorcised, quickly
    trodden upon
in their swell and surge of rebellious tide;
repenting the sweet treachery of Satan,
she flays the alphabet
into its proper reverence of kneeling,
she cringes it into words of praise.

Bonum est confiteri,
for yea, the Lord is her lover
and her glad garden's pollen,
inhaled as though an addiction,
celebrates how she is taken,
how she prospers in His grapple;
then sweat baptizes her trance
beneath its boiling waves
as she mumbles out the vows of her condition,
enjoining God to take care
as He impales her with His joy:

Jubilato Deo - consummatum est!

Limp in her seized convulsions,
then leaping and dancing
in her internal and blazing corrugations
of a thousand postures,
she screams out to her Lord God;
she calls Him by His unknown first name,
drowns in a gloried profanity of secret juices
and, in a vulgate passion, she erupts,
recalling The Flood.

But her tide recedes
in flight from her treacherous moon:

Beati immaculati—
Pure and shriven, she gropes at her plantings,
her imprisoned hot house, her green garden;
as though a robot of burning flesh,
she drops an embryo of alien seed
and with the window-light let in,
she sings internal chants,
hard translations
of the only songs Saint Joan could hear.

For Mary Frances Finnegan,
who stared into the haunted
mirror and took holy vows.

"Batter my heart, three-person'd
God . . ."

-John Donne
Divine Poems XIV.

There is no theological plumbing
to fix the leak in seminal pipes.
-Lufwalnu Nabru-Orgen.

In Camera

In the darkness, I tell him
of my seeping fluids when
I envision Sister Hilaire unclad,
her moral symmetry nude,
stripped of her habit's camouflage,
a naked Susannah
dreamed in the ruins of her fortress vows.

Hidden in his see-through blind,
the young priest must feel his
cassock tremble, his surplice shamed;
throbbing with fret,
he must listen to the gross ventriloquist
of my sodden dreams;
although masked behind his scrim,
I can sense his mute mea culpas
for us both,
unwashed of sweat
in this flimsy locker-room
where I dare him to know the rude rhythms
of sin's concussive glory
beneath the cover of whatever is beneath;
he and I hear the same treacherous sirens singing
as seduction spills its furtive flood
in otherwise Saharan loins
where smirking stains define a crude blemish,
a snickering Rorschach.

The wedding to Jesus cannot work,
the pipes will always leak with life
and drown the prim grammar of the Word;
the scalpel slashes among
neutered thighs that still must quiver
when the plain beauty of nuns
arsons at desire.

As the seminary hand-book instructs,
he asks: "Have you sinned, my son?":
Of course, so I mutter out my trespass
in all its seminal plurals;
with a smirking malice, I recite each detail.
"My son," indeed; this from arid loins;
such monastic deceits become
more worthy of Cardinal Wolsey,
naked to his useful loves
before his jealous peers
begrudged his foresaken vows.

My confessor,
beardless,
barely risen from his ordination,
must have fended off Mary's Seven Dolors,
telling beads to curse Voltaire.

Shriven and admonished,
I leave him in the rubble
of his turmoil
and his revival of some ancient Latin glory
to comfort his harried suppositions.

Paris and Lugano in the swelter of an
August day, circa 1994.
MBcMW

old soldiers never die; their privates just fade away.

Graffito on a wall.

WAR

Note:

Normandy, in the Summer of 1944, remains one trenchant and stinking tenant in the memory of my nose. The hedgerow country was full of apple orchards which had been brutalized by artillery. Apples and the bodies of cows rotted in the sun. Bees were everywhere and flies formed dark clouds as they scavenged. Cows seemed uncertain as they browsed. Sweat, cow-dung, blood, death and noise, in their harsh competition, all have a special stink. In the midst of it all, French farmers, moving as stoics, were seen trampling huge vats of apples which would make that paralyzing potion known as Calvados. One drink helped all of us move forward under optimum sedation of fear, if not immunity, through the soft apple slush, the dung and the bodies we used to know.

Beach-Heads

Run, my sons, on soft sea sand,
find the perfect echo-shell:
On friendly beaches and on fair land,
find your heaven and your hell.

Note:

Baby-dolls and tiny prams prepare prepubescent females for the rituals and bondage of marriage and baby-bearing, if not for sex. Toy guns and bloody tales of cruel heroism harden the infant male for the inevitable fate of war and his expected role in it. The terrors of combat are transmuted from the base ore of their stink and hurt into some star-spangled drama of patriotism. One nurses at the breast of The Flag; civic vitamins are fed by American Legion nurses, whose beribboned parades are staged to teach the young the glory of dying young. The avoidance of war is condemned as the evil of peace-mongering and draft-dodging.

How can anyone doubt that the Big National Brother who watches over us, is a sadistic general, gleaming with medals? He clutches Klausewitz in one hand and with the other, he holds aloft his black maps that are marked in red with every short-cut along the Road To Samara.

One needs eternal youth to outrace the stealth of time. How sad that my sons will never be able to run fast enough.

-Brucius Africanus Pacificus.

1944

JUNE 6, 7, 8, 9, 10, 11, 12, 13, 14, 15
16, 17, 18, 19, 20, 21, 22, 23, 24, 25, 26,
27, 28, 29, 30; July 1, 2, 3, etc.

St. Lo, St. Mere Église.

Normandy in the summer of 1944 remains one trenchant aromatic tenant in the memory of my nose and brain. The hedgerow landscape was partitioned into orchards brutalized by bombardment from the air and artillery from the sea. Apples and the bodies of cows rotted in the sun. Bees and flies competed in dark clouds, as they scavenged. Those cows that lived appeared confused as they stumbled in their personal browse. Sweat, dung, noise and death had their own special confusion and stink.

In the midst of all the clamor of my portion of the chaos, now and then, French farmers, moving like wound-up stoics, could be seen trampling huge vats of crushed apples as they made that paralyzing potion known as Calvados. One drink of that merciful anesthesia helped us all move forward under the maximum sedation of fear, if not immunity. Bent, burdened and vulnerable, we sloshed through the fallen apples, the dung and the bodies we used to know.

M·I·L·L·E·N·N·I·U·M

gather all
the nervous
pieces,
twitching ganglia
and gore;
medicate
the melancholy,
there is
nothing more.

Note:

Christ and Mahatma Gandhi are said to have been apostles of peace and propagandists for theories of human love and its mythical possibilities. Both Gandhi and Christ suffered violent deaths, victims of hate. Under the circumstances of our present stage of what is called Civilization, it would be advisable that Christ put off indefinitely His rumored promise of a Second Coming. If he comes as a pacifist, he will be suspect and ridiculed. If he comes urging love, He may be confused with alien gurus and other counterfeiters of pseudo-magic. In the garb painted upon Him by artists he might be sneered at as a Beatnick. More menacing, however, would be the focus of American Legion and Pentagon Strangeloves.

On the other hand, if He returns as a warrior, He might desecrate the very faith that is derived from his name and which promises salvation, not death everlasting. Indeed, the world is so deeply mired in faeces that the most useful role for His humility might be as a Wiper of the Collective Sphincter. He might also find it useful to learn how to walk on shit, or how to avoid Merde In The First Degree.

I remember distinctly the tired tumult of my urges
and the sun shining, and the dust, and the clouds,
and how I turned my rifle down.

I remember a cow, dumb and heedless in the street
and a woman sweeping dung,
while Prague and Pilsen were just some kilometers
out of sight.

I recall that songs were sung,
attention stood,
allegiance re-asserted
and I saw two colonels cry.
There was a first night of awkward peace
sleeping with pillows trimmed in Bohemian lace
and letters that admonished me to sleep well.
I hugged them into humanity
and trembled and felt quite old.

How distant is any day
and how many hurts away?

But, there were Prague and Pilsen,
and I,
having dug holes in history,
I was stretched out alive
on the same continent with Paris,
just some wars and worlds removed
from Miss Upjohn's geography and P. S. 89,
and all the things she could never teach me.
I remember though that she told me
that Sheffield made fine cutlery,
that coals were dug at Newcastle
and drydocks launched ships at Southampton:
I should have known that France had beaches,
that Normandy must have been noted
for this or that,

plus D-Day, Plus One, Plus Two, Plus et cetera,
and divers deadly things from St. Lo to Metz.
I should have known that France
had military aliases such as Omaha and Utah,
American Indian hinterlands,
but as French as Bar-Le-Duc.

However, Miss Upjohn was a virgin,
she shied away from flesh and French facts,
she disapproved of certain acts:

Between us, there can be no bond,
now that I can teach Upjohn.

VE DAY - 1945,
Germany

Love Song

If I call beyond the groping of my echo,
go breathless through the stench
of recent heroism;
If I can immunize my close contortion
and defeat the angry purpose of some hedge,
what deranged category
claims this pattern of my hazard,
this hostile moment of reprieve . . .?

How shall I remark this portion of my burden,
this duty of a peaceful pledge,
and how engage some masked and restless hill?
With the quick insistence of the hour,
I must exorcise all sadness
to the distance
away from where the anxious wait to grieve.

But here, it grows dark;
the night has crashed among the orchards
where light-years
come between the senses
and the mortal thunder.

Tomorrow will be different,
I shall gather blossoms from the broken boughs
as I wander in the vacuum of an interlude
where the baffled cows are lost among the
flies and stink,
and I stumble out of kinship with the brutes.

Tomorrow, I shall gather blossoms, weave a
wreath
and wonder who will weave my own.

It is well, this interlude;
I gaze upon the ranks of captured foe
and look away to where hasty heaps of stone
mound the land and mark a cross.
And if I call beyond the groping of my echo,
who will say or hear?

29 August, France
1944

Before They Drop (An Army Day Parade)

Before they drop,
They are as doomed as the dead
Who marched to these same requiems
Before they played at angry hide-and-seek
Upon some wet and coded shore;
Before their sweat of marching dries
Or the hoarseness of the cheering goes
To make way for more loyal cries,
They will be daggered in their rows;
And those now becoming in their human seed
Will grow to learn the making of their oath and tread,
And loyal cheers will urge them on
With loyalty to join the dead,
Then,
We who scavenge in all the wondrous words of praise,
And plant the passion of our cause,
Will weed among the murder of our crop.

It was 1942, a time of Roosevelt's Four Delicious Freedoms (the cause that refreshes). It was a time of passionate vows to liberate Europe from the yoke of Nazi racism. And, in this fair land, stolen from the Indians by English Puritans, brave lads marched off in hot pursuit of doom. They were much too late, of course, to save six million Jews, but had plenty of time to segregate blacks in Jim Crow battalions of liberation. So much for democracy and its rusty ironies.

R·I·T·U·A·L·S

Summon men of every cloth
bringing lotions, tapers, vessels,
to whisper lyric choruses
for the burial of wrath;

Sift the marrow,
smooth the bone,
glands, pores, the tearless moisture,
all assembled
in a proper posture;

Light the candles, fill a chalice,
mark the manufactured prayer:

Hail, the conquered hero comes,
shattered into unknown sums,
fractured into decimals.

Now a pious intonation,
now the gesture and the symbol;
fix a flare within an orbit
and sprinkle shrapnel on each place.

When I Was Trapped by History

When I was trapped by history
and caught up in its mystery
of international protocol,
I thought I'd understand it all.
I always knew life's shallow shapes
were like little foxes, minus grapes,
but diplomatic hocus-pocus
had never swum into my focus,
like simple, fundamental things,
to wit: green cabbages and kings.
I almost understood the need for war,
though not what men like fighting for;
sleeping in the rain and mud
and wasting other people's blood
are basic, not too complicated,
as the many dead have indicated.
War lets us piously chip our stone
to honor shattered flesh and bone;
we have statues stenographed
and marble memory epitaphed—
memorials to distant pain
where we say none has died in vain.
And now, we bravely huddle here,
running from our fear of fear,
But can you fathom what's going on
in the Councils pro and con?
We must have done these things before
we fought the other recent war.

Heldenleben Peasant
Circa 1946

CRUCIAL FICTIONS

In Jesus' Presence Did I Weep

In Jesus' presence did I weep
When His English-speaking vicar
Touched holy tears about my head
And pacified me into semblance of the dead.
Although I slept, the only dreams were had
By those awake in one of God's cathedral houses.
There, clean-conceived priests were met
To execute the rituals of the sabbath day;
There, they rubbed the Scriptures
Like Aladdin's Lamp,
And watched the magic of the Faith, its terror,
Come burdened in the shape of conscience
For all the definitions of all imagined sins.
And in that gothic manger where I lay,
Asleep and black, all covered warm
In every Sunday silk and satin of the Proper Word,
My comforts were the bleeding jewels of His
weeping,
Distilled from the abcess of His wounds,
Codified in the Book of Common Prayer,
Sealed within the text of hope.
And there, never once,
As held bosomed in that glowing creche,
Where the sun set sudden fire
To the fables of the saints postured in leaded glass,
Never once did I dream
That in all of life,
As in all of death,
Our feet are bound,
Our bodies pierced.

In answer to the make-believe recitals of The Word
By immaculate curates of my flesh,
Lean out of heaven, O, Jesus Christ,
Delivered from Your Roman hurts,

And speak to all who sleep or wake in cradles,
For we are here,
As all advices tell, in sin,
Behind the bars of Adam's seed,
Wounded sore by the secret wish and every pitied need,
For no candles lit up our passage from the womb -
We cane in darkness, as Gospels took You from the Tomb.
And so, for all of us,
The sleeping and the woke,
Who gesture in some pantomime of grace,
Who by communion make vows and weddings to
    the Host,
There is need,
As Holy Books are mute,
To know the census of that place
Where You have risen
And whether souls at one in death
Accept their salvage from a Jew.

Note:

Thoughts of a black infant at his christening, as he broods upon the predicament of a Christian society that hates Jews and admires German industry. Both predicament and ironic dilemma are intensified when it is realized that most of the Biblical patriarchs and saints are Jewish. Do they ever wonder about the dogma and how it was first inscribed on the Hebrew scrolls? The only justification for this kind of faithful aberration is the belief that God, a white Protestant, has to be born again, since He cuckolded Joseph in an affair with Mary.

Pieties

The genuflections of the humble,
Accompanied by sacred mumble,
Echo beneath each gothic dome
Of all the roads that lead to Rome;
Yet, life is albatross and omen,
Alike for Protestant or Roman:
Tell Dear God, or tell a bead
And still remains the hungry need.

Tiger Options

I, dry image,

All arranged,

Recline in satin ceremony;

I, the spiced, cosmetic mummy,

The once-removed, well-dressed shell,

Am now resplendent with the favorite bloom

Of certain heirs;

I, with the internals of my doom

Autopsied into vials and lore,

Make this last appearance

As though hesitating on the sill

Of an ancient and obscene riddle,

Or, as though condemned to choose

Between two dungeon doors;

I, alone,

With folded hands,

Must now decipher old intrigue

And, like a certain legend's lover,

Go with cuckold advice and nod

To some tiger or to God.

Wanderings along The Road To Samara.

The True Faith

Some orthodox wear yarmulkes,
Some Christians sport a cross:
I wonder which imagined God
Is absolutely Boss.

Lufwalnu Nabru-Orgen
Heretic Farms, Belly Acres,
Hell Gate, N.Y.

B. Wright, Who Would
Rather B. Rich.
Anno Domini??????

Catherine's Wheel

Aunt Catherine fingers her rosary
and mumbles a clavichord of songs
to her three lovers.
In ridicule of my flight from God,
she warns that when death's flames
light hell within my brain,
I, too, will welcome her trinity,
seek to undo my Sunday truancies
and flex stubborn bone to beg of the Holy Ghost,
et al. a saving grace.

Captured by her thrall, she recreates
the doomed pageant of Calvary,
marks the air with sharp angles of the Crucifix,
re-condemns the Roman spears,
adds me to the sacred rota of St. Jude,
and rejoices that her soul has fled all fears.

ii

Aunt Catherine, in the large fullness of her flesh,
nightly blocked my bedroom door
with God's vigilance;
never agile in my kneeling, I nevertheless
made the posture she enjoined,
closed my eyes and sought in vain
to clasp a vision in my mind.
I was programmed in my bedtime repetitions,
compelled by loving oppression
to address her triple icons,
all certified by priest and pope.
Thus bent to reluctant duty,
I alerted God to bless my aunt
and ease her smiting
in the passion of belief
and see in me at least some virtues of The Good Thief.

iii

Pressed and shined for my cruel
sanctuary (domine refugiam),

I wait upon the immaculate shepherds of the Savior
and waste the Sabbath as a servant at the altar.
Aunt Catherine in the knelt aerobics of her prayer,
moves her lips and fondles beads
in mute communication.
On Monday morning, promptly at eight,
she will commit my soul and brain
to the Sisters of the Sacred Mercy
where I shall be scathed and rebuked by both The
    Word and rod
as I am taught the rote mysteries of the love of God.

iv

The year is filled with Sabbaths,
holy names and days of obligation;
given pennies for my tribute to the Virgin,
I buy candy on the way to salvation,
as Aunt Catherine lies ill on the
Second Sunday before Lent. She is unhealed by the
cheerful invocations of Father Indelicata.
Still, she smiles as the faith shapes her lips
to pronounce the syllables of *exultate, justi,*
benedic, anima mea. Later, I shall be alone,
unbound. Temptation will be the guide in which I
    trust
as I invest a portion of God's meager tithe
and prepare to mouth confession and atonement.
As with a drunken priest, my transfiguration
must abide internal inquisitions -
but not just yet.
And when the kept promise of doom's deliverance
confronts my time,
somewhere, Aunt Catherine will hear my
repetition of The Word,
and then, with anxious mea culpas stammered out,
I will wrestle in the havoc of my doubt.

The Christian holidays are always cold - Lent, Easter,
Christmas, are times when Jesus becomes the faith's best-
selling fiction, allowing toy ghosts to haunt the shabby
house of reality. Having walked on water, the Second
Coming will see Christ walking on *merde.*

God Burns His Words Upon Our Sight

God burns His words upon our sight,
Allows the Middle Ages, through long-time minstrels
To sing Trappist lections of His gentle might,
While the tears of Christ
Daily irrigate our arid dooms and jokes.
If only God's hand at His easel could compete
With della Robbia's angels and Rembrandt's revelations;
If only the graffiti of His patriarchs could match the writings
Which once stunk with truth on the subway toilet walls.
But then, had the Gauls not lost long-division to Caesar;
Had Hannibal never lost his elephants and won the long hike,
The Mediterranean's melanin would have survived what
    the Romans lost.
Let us then, on occasion pray and ponder as we touch
And feel the unnamed shapes
Climbing behind Modigliani's skies,
For we welcome the easel's sweet deception
And the deceived mind's arrogance made securely right
With matters which it masks with much disguise
Through which the empty battles of the past arise.
Brave legions of foot and horse ail and ache in my sleep
Both in their dust and death giving God the losses of His sheep.

ii

It is Christmas once again, a time of famous feasts;
The woods of Birnam are captured in the room
Where toys and ghosts of toys are spread
And we make children of our minds;
We sit among the moving figures we have wound,
Pursuing a child's emotion on a winter merry-go-round.
We can hear the icy pipes, the harsh asthma of their sound
As the frozen organ of the carousel
Beats a pace for the rigid wildness of its wooden zoo.
Painted horses pump their riders up and down
While flashing lights make alloyed tinsel gleam;
Clinging to their naked steeds,

The children condense upon the air the steam of life's
      suggestion,
Spin in perfect circles, clutch their beasts
And marvel at the lacquered white of snow.
Outside the park, they marvel at the marvels of the frosted
      scene,
Where otherwise retired men
Beg good deeds and supervise red paper chimneys
As they act and ring the bells of December's Hallowe'en.
The children see that one old Santa has the sneezes and a
      running nose,
But treats are all and tricks forgotten
In the fire of beads and neon flakes
Flashing silver and with holly-red.
All this pretty pageant, sprinkled with bursting horns
Of candied brittle-chew and ribboned sweets
Tempt the City's speeding Magi racing through the streets.
Only the children wish to pause and hear the uniformed
      Salvationists
Playing trumpets in the cold,
Or gaze upon the glowing creches in the windows,
The sparkling bottles wrapped in swaddling foil
And know the urgency of nights before they spoil.
The snow makes a new ecology. The world is white.
Who remembers now any scene or sight
When Jamestown was an un-sought port
And black Africa found a darker night
Among Christians and their sacred sport?

The Dead Sea Scrolls

As through a veil of moving water
We know the Festivals of Light and Ember;
We mix our sacraments and sin
In exegeses of our faith
And look upon the primates' crosses
As guardians of an empty cell,
And we catechize each sense of Hell
And confess our moral losses.
Still, under the omens of Corpus Christi,
Assumption and rogation,
My love and I have made our signs,
We have worn the ash
And tasted bitter;
For we, schooled in the advent of seasons,
Know, also, the passion of atonement;
All lections of the Body and of the Blood,
And we know all saints and all souls
Are one with God
And each deciphered Scroll.

1955, In Hell's Kitchen

On Sermons For The Dead

La Tentative de L'Impossible
On The Obsequies For The Late Oliver Sutton
A Recollection Of Forgotten Memories of Life
The Gestures of the Faith; The Words of Man
Amid The Well-Dressed Absence of God.

How like an actor doth the vicar look,
Blessing chalice, candle, book;
A thousand times hath he rehearsed
To banish demons he has cursed;
The lesser priests, all dressed in drag
Know how and when their knees must sag
To genuflect before the cross,
Acknowledging Jesus Christ as Boss.
Dr. Weston pontificates,
But his voice is false and grates;
Resplendent in his gold and black
With blazed devices on his back,
His equatorial black forebears
Would be amazed by his haughty airs;
This Afro-Saxon priestly scribe
Has no memory of his tribe,
And yet, the place and pageantry and rites,
Incense, thurible and candle lights,
Are those The Duppy Man addressed,
As pagans in the nude confessed.

ii

The naked jungle, now far remote
Has been exchanged for cape and coat,
With Roman collars at the neck
To match epistles and collect
And mumble *Domino confido*
And trust the alien stranger's credo;
Here, Blacks worship with pious plea,

Far from their Middle-Passage sea;
Once slave and owner in their thrall,
Both answer now the same God's call;
Full-blown, as though from darkness hurled,
Blacks no longer are Third World;
They imitate the speech and ways
Of those who owned their other days,
And when they genuflect and bend,
Both intone the same Amen.
Alas, that sterile hymns and songs
Can cover up all Christian wrongs
And Pentecostal glee and shouts
Form no part of faith and doubts;
'As the Episcopalian mouth intones,
The Blacks become their whitest clones.'

A Day In The Death Of . . .
Tuesday, July 19th, 1983
B. Wright, Urban Heathen.

Black is what the prisons are
in their stagnate count of hours,
Made the total of all time,
Creeping in each perjured heart,
Made bitter in a vulgar rhyme.
Made bitter on the walls.

Black is where dark devils dance
With time within
Black genesis,
Then it pirouettes
A crippled orbit in a trance
And crawls beneath, below the flesh
Where darkness goes its way.

Black is where dry deserts burn,
The Niger and the Congo flow,
From where The Middle Passage went
With Fulani, Ibo and captured Hausa
To English faith and Puritans
And places conscience cannot go.

Black is where thatched temples burned
Incense to my kinship's hurt,
Where traders shaped my father's pain,
His name, his person and his place
Among dead figures in a frieze,
In the spectrum of his race.

At a United Nations Reception

In too severely tailored suits,
The Africans are distanced from their roots;
Impeccable, each consul stands,
Proud in the independence of once-cap-
tured lands;
But Europeans still hold hypnotic away,
Dictating what and how to say;
Equatorial mother tongues
Do not betray the mouth or lungs;
Every delegate who speaks
To tell the world what each one seeks,
Makes no mention, small or grand
Of languages from his native land;
Just why they ignore their dialects
In spoken word and alien texts,
Baffles history, confuses race
And tells us something of their place.
The northern whites who conquered them
And looted precious ore and gem,
Called them nigger, boy, and worse
And left them with an empty purse.

Afro-Saxons in their dress,
They've learned to pray and how to bless;
Their animistic gods are dead
And Jesus troubles in each head;
Missionaries no longer need fear
That they, as food, will disappear;
Where once the totem pole was all,
Churches now sound a foreign call;
White shadows stain each dark cause,
Black freedom and black national laws;
Ancient rituals are now abhored
As tribal mores are ignored,
When Third World diplomats convene

To show the evolution of each hybrid gene;
Hypocrisy and tact both merge
As manners quash each native urge;
Politesse is all the rule
In this well-dressed, cautious school;
Blacks smile at whites who stole their wealth
And drink martinis to their health;
How shall I tell the World that's Third
That it and the First are both absurd?

Note:

At a cocktail party sponsored by the Nigerian Ambassador to that ethnic mélange on the East River known as the United Nations, on a cold February evening in 1982, where the only person wearing a dashiki [made in Japan], was an American black, who somehow imagined he was mixing with "brothers."

In My Life, The Rude Ironic

In my life, the rude ironic
truth is my sardonic
perverse imp,
who will sit and simp,
then suddenly reveal
with depths I seldom feel,
delineations of a friend
who met a paradoxic end
while conferring on a truce
[you know that diplomatic noose];
to mention such a thing
gives conciliation sting.

Now, you take the case of Mr. Jason,
who was 33 degrees of Mason;
his closet held the choicest suits,
he only wore hand-crafted boots;
his underwear was London-shaped
and when his red-lined cape was draped,
his waxed moustache and head were Greek,
a Praxiteles that could breathe and speak;
he knew each ancient tale of Gaul
and how all empires thrive and fall;
he knew of Vercingétorix
and he read in Sanskrit just for kicks;
he'd memorised Gibbon's Decline and Fall,
Aeschuylus, Plato—he knew them all;
quotations from Maimonides
were uttered with consummate ease,
and he was modern, too, quite up-to-date;
he knew of Churchill's Hinge of Fate,
each famous duchess, knight or lord,
Picasso, Joyce, Ford Maddox Ford—
they were first names within his circle,
including the Barrymores and Una Merkle;
they sought his approval for their scripts;

Cunard and Cooke would book no trips
without some wisdom from his lips;
magnetic poles declined to pull
and no Pope would dare to seal a bull,
without petitions prayed to him
to win the favour of his whim;
the House of Lords, the Nine Old Men,
denied relief, lest he say when;
blacks and whites did not dare riot
if Mr. Jason shushed them quiet;
no radar-scope or Laser Beam
could ever be just what they seem,
unless dear Jason gave his permission
for science to follow its condition;
if Zodiacal Signs confused
biographies that had been used,
Mr. Jason, speaking *ex cathedra*,
could rehabilitate even poor Phaedra,
Medusa, the Gorgons and even Mephisto,
or make a king of Monte Cristo;
he absolved the Gentiles of their libel
that corrupted gospels of the Bible;
he knew the Roman deicide
and how the papal councils lied-
except for John The Twenty-Third,
that Honest Keeper of the herd;
he could convert the thieves of Tunis
or mollify the young DeFunis
by making him enroll in CORE
and praise George Schuyler's *Black No More!*
Smokers were convinced to switch
while fleas forgot to cause an itch;
the rudest oaf would prosper couth
and even Nixon tell the truth;
rivers, also, would reverse their flow
if Mr. Jason wished it so.

But with all of Jason's runic magic,
his Achilles' heel made him tragic,

for despite the miracles he had wrought,
he failed to win what he'd long sought:
He was not able to embrace
and heal the bitterness of race,
and absent that, his staff and rod
were impotent to make him God;
but neither Jason nor the True Faith's Lord
could solve the enigmas of discord
between the blacks and whites in life
or know how they should annul all strife.

Face the fact, there is no Savior
who can cope with color and its behavior;
so let us caution the amazing Mr. Jason,
despite his status as an exalted Mason,
while God, Jesus and the Holy Ghost
can take their sacred pomp and boast
to Mr. Alighieri's fires,
there to dwell with false-faced liars
like Reverend Ike, or Billy Graham,
or Uncle Sam in Viet Nam.
The Trinity's wafer and its watered wine
do not match the passion of Father Divine,
or Daddy Grace, or Prophet Jones,
or Pentecostal store-front moans;
The College of Cardinals and Vincent Peale
make their presence less than real
when compared with what life tells
of distant heavens and pressing hells.

But no Jason functions in a void,
anymore than Dr. Freud,
or seminarians of the Dead Sea Scrolls,
or troglodytes or midget trolls,
for not worse than Aimee Semple McPherson
was Jason in his flesh and person,
so when we step through Alice's Looking Glass,
or smoke a joint of cannabis grass
or seek out Omar's tent for quiet balm
and his serene narcotic calm,

I will always praise each flamboyant Jason
and the sweet illusions that they hasten:
And when I lay me down to slumber,
I'll dream that Jason calls my number.

Obiter Dictum:

This is doggerel in the manger, as we wait for Godot.
While it is not quite stable, there is no intention to stall.
Originally entitled Jason And The Golden Faeces, I
assumed arguendo, that if I were to remain on an even keel,
I had to take a stern course, Oar-Lock myself securely into
what Dylan Thomas has aptly referred to as the poet's "sullen
craft." At least the foregoing is not beyond anyone's depth
and is easy to fathom. If I seem shallow, remember that he
also surfs who only stands and wades.

Lufwalnu Nabru-Nolef,
Also Known As
Brucius Labirt Africanus, CXVIII
December 31, 1974,
Hard By St. Surplice, Paris.

Neuroses are red,
Melancholia is blue;
I'm schizophrenic:
What are you?

Totem and Tabu or Not Tabu

For All of Those in Huts or Palaces
Who Have to Undergo Analysis

Does it matter, does it matter,
If my shirt and collar tatter?
Suppose my one suit has a hole,
Or suppose I catch a common cold:

Does it matter, really matter,
Whether I am thin or fatter?

Suppose my shoes are wearing thin,
Suppose my feet more out than in;
Suppose my coat is torn and frayed,
Suppose my rent remains unpaid:

Does it really, really matter,
If it's both the first and latter?

Suppose my mouth needs costly
    dentures,
Suppose my faithless misadventures
Come before some magistrate
And I am dealt some awful fate:

Does it, can it, really matter,
Such inconsequential data?

Suppose I'm Good and pray to God
And cultivate the barren sod;
Suppose I call all men my brothers
And do to them as I'd have others
Do unto me all the year—
Would you think me rather queer?

But, does it, tell me, really matter,
If dreams are only dreamed to shatter?

Suppose I like to lose Lost Causes;
Suppose I write symbolic clauses
And call them poetry-though minor-
But think that little else is diviner:
Matter, come, tell me, really matter,
Whether I am saint or satyr?

Suppose I know what's Good,
    what's Bad
And yet, I feel the Truth's been had;
Suppose my psyche is schizo-manic
(I crush gnats and love a panic);
Suppose I stretch out on a bed
And speak the dreams from which
    I've fled;
Suppose I fill a phallic void
With symptoms from Adler, Jung
    and Freud:

Does it, can it, come now, really matter,
Although libido warms my chatter?

Suppose I feel that Dr. Kinsey
Has written text that really pins me
Underneath some hush-hush complex-
Suppose I'm doubtful of my sex!
Suppose some sphincter-pubic token
Defines my hurt when toilet broken;
Suppose I dream a dream of tunnels
Shaped like perforated funnels;
Suppose my consciousness is teeming
With all the dreams I feared of
    dreaming;
Suppose all geophysics are racial
And civil rights are interspatial;
Suppose that outer-space is fated
To be the only world that's integrated;
Suppose I dream of signs and symbols

And needles piercing heart-shaped
    thimbles;
Does it really, tell me, matter
When I hear the wistful patter
Of my steps re-tracing life
To the womb of my father's wife?

Written by a Jung patient on a couch,
Where Super-Ego and Id scream ouch!
And where arrogance loses imagined power
And pays a toll that's by the hour.

Done in Paris, Circa some other time,
By B. Wright And His Other Selves.

Bangs and Whimpers

When Man Shakes Spear, Or Spear Shakes Man, Or, The Will By
Which We Live, Or, The First Will Was The Last Will, Or, Much
Ado About Living On Bard Time

As one may not know, The Pun is a Noble Art;
Now this does not mean that every IQ plays a noble part
In making puns the aristocracy of syntax,
For quite the contrary are the ambiguity-ridden facts.
Some artists paint their puns from neologistic, chameleon easels,
Like a Witch of Endor, Rorschached with smeary measels,
And Hieronymous Bosch, the famous free-flinging and flippant
     Fleming,
Who condemned with josh and joshed condemning;
And then, of course, take the brilliant case of William Shakespeare,
Who knew that life was mixed and meddled, quivering, quaint
     and queer;
He knew, too, foibled frauds that foreran Freud's knowing life is
     teeming
With monstrous matters more or less real than all that they
     were seeming.

Recall, if you will, Vienna's vile vice and the mad moods of
     Measure For Measure,
That rare-perfect tense and tensile text of etymological treasure,
Dipped in dryly droll double-meaning and sinful, subtle punning,
Wherein, in a maze of non-synthetic and sheer syntactical cunning,
The brilliant, balding, bearded Bard defined how, incognito, we
     can see
That taunting traitor, Truth, behind the souls of what all seemers
     seem to be;
If you have seen Scene Three, which Scene, once seen,
Can be seen as not obscene, you see it mean
The mean and meaningless meanings of losing lost, un-lasting
     life itself,
Whether painfully pauperous, or counterfeit with the gilded,
     gelded guilt of pelf;

But I do not mean mean to mean a Manichean manic means,
And by no means deprived and destitute of the patent purpose
    of purpled pun-paeans;
Nor do I suggest something stingy, stodgy, sterile or gross,
Or even bare-boned, as with Poor Yorick's skinless skull and
    un-fleshed ghost,
Nor even some indeterminate or intermediate place,
As with Othello trapped in his dark black race,
Nor even that mean of Perihelion,
And never the upside-down image of Thessaly-in-Pelion,
But only that mean which means its own intent
And intends to mean only what is meant;
Thus, the nimble nobility of punning's meaningful art
Elevates mystic miens and makes for the meaning of both soul
    and heart,
For, in languished life, we are all scroungers and angst-filled gleaners.
Whether as geriatric antiquarians, or passionate, hedonistic teeners;
We learn that we secrete then exude secrets, but not their
    common comprehension,
And so secrets remain secret of their substance, but never of their
    too-much mention.
But enough now of this poor brooding on the rich word-play
    of Good Will,
For goodwill bids me to make me mute and to be both good and still:
And so to bed, with much unsaid,
Knowing that where there is a Will, he has saved our every day
And that he left not muchly much for us to too-much say.

And keep in mind that:
    Neuroses are red,
    Melancholia is blue;
    I'm schizophrenic -
    What are you?

B. Wright, Who Would
Rather Be

This is the way the world ends
This is the way the world ends
This is the way the world ends
Not with a bang but a whimper.
—T.S. Eliot.

MAUNDERINGS

Sub-committees on submarines
Do not subsist on rye and beans;
Prime ministers can preen and primp
And stuff themselves on murdered shrimp,
While Commonwealth talks
With all its races
All fumble with look-alike attache cases;

Aides-de-camp
Write complex speeches
Ignoring lessons which history teaches;
The underdeveloped embassies
Are seeming-rich and posh and grand
For every poor and stricken land;

Secretaries with titled doors
Have time to fornicate upon their floors,
While portfolios
With Plans for Peace
Wait for wars and life to cease;

Conference rooms hear loud debates
On lebensraum and ancient hates;
The dignitaries in starch and vests,
Decry Pacific atom tests;
The Four World Powers nod their heads,
Including Russia's well-dressed Reds;

Shall we bomb or shall we pause
In making war our peaceful cause?

The Viet-Cong and their guerrillas
Are not the only careful killers;
Supersonic jets and crews
Conspire in melancholy news;

The Presidents who command the wars
Are very much like pious whores,
Who hate to sin
Though do it well,
Seducing peace while wed to hell.

An organ grinder
On any corner
Can crank a tune for every mourner;
Weeping monkeys
Can pluck at fate
Producing runes of love and hate;
But what of Peace
And what of war,
And soldier-visas to some angry shore?

A Green Beret
Without a head
Confirms the presence of the dead;

In Viet Nam
A burning priest
Attests the passion of the East;
The answer of the learned West
Blows in the wind of each protest:

Oh, what is Peace,
The soldiers cry,
But the bang and whimper when we die?

———————————

Perhaps this should have parodied a title of Wallace
Stevens, by being called *THE EMPEROR OF I SCREAM*.
Originally, this was a brood concerned with Jay Moss, a vio-
lent and implacable agent of Peace, a stander of vigils, who
took his conscience to a Federal jail, where he suffered in
durance vile for his refusal to serve as a brute-vassal in uni-
form. It is my memorandum, also, to those who must make
reluctant landfall on hostile beaches. Since death is a banal-
ity, the unavoidable penalty for allowing life to begin, it may
be disjunctively remembered that, They Also Surf Who Only
Stand And Wade. Thus the banality. And so to death.